Presents

Ancestors in a Nation Divided

An In-Depth Guide to
Researching Your Civil War Ancestors

by Cindy Freed

Published by The In-Depth Genealogist, Utica, Ohio.

Edited by Jennifer M. Alford and Terri O'Connell

Photographs provided by Cindy Freed

Cover design by Jennifer M. Alford

www.TheInDepthGenealogist.com

Dedication

This book is dedicated to my great-great grandfather George Washington Lowery. It was his military service with Company A 81st Pennsylvania Volunteer Infantry during the Civil War that set my research in motion. With little more than his name, his courageous service inspired me to read, research and investigate his place in our country's history. It is my hope that this book honors him, his service and his memory.

Table of Contents

Introduction

The Civil War is probably the most engrossing event in our country's history. Men were willing to risk their life for what they believed in, families were fractured as they took opposite sides, cities and states splintered into rival factions. It's a compelling time. It's also an emotional time for everyone that lived during that era and that same emotion has carried through to generations today. We are fortunate that private and public entities have done a remarkable job sustaining this heritage through battlefield and landmark preservation easily making remnants of the Civil War accessible to all. All this makes us wonder where did our ancestors fit in?

I was introduced to my Civil War ancestor a good number of years ago. Succinctly put great-great grandfather George Washington Lowery served with an Ohio regiment. That was it. Those few words were all I knew about my veteran ancestor. That was the extent of his legacy handed down in my family. I was satisfied with this small amount of information for years until I visited Gettysburg on a cool October day a few years ago. Listening to the audio tour I bought in the gift shop I was amazed at how I was completely drawn into the emotion of each appointed stop. I could visualize and sense soldiers, average guys, standing shoulder to shoulder charging the enemy. Farmers, laborers, shop keepers falling to bullets, regrouping, pain, cheers, death and maybe victory. My visit to Gettysburg was filled with such an overwhelming emotional reaction to what had happened there that I needed to know where my ancestor fit into the Civil War picture.

This book is the result of research into my great-great grandfather's military service in the Civil War. (I subsequently found he fought with a Pennsylvania regiment not one in Ohio.) This is a guide for any genealogist or family historian who wants to concentrate some research time on their ancestor's Civil War experience. I hope it's a helpful tool as you learn about your ancestor's role in the Civil War.

Chapter One

Beginning Your Civil War Research

"In all of us there is a hunger, marrow-deep, to know our heritage- to know who we are and where we have come from. Without this enriching knowledge, there is a hollow yearning. No matter what our attainments in life, there is still a vacuum, an emptiness, and the most disquieting loneliness." - Alex Haley, Roots

With the observance of the 150th anniversary of the Civil War we have seen commemorations of various battles on the nightly news or even attended events locally. Remembering the bloody battle at Antietam or the widely known battle at Gettysburg piques our interest in life during that time. The continuing programs and events that pay tribute to those men who served may have prompted you to wonder whether your ancestor had a part in one of the most significant events in our country's history. If your ancestors lived in this country during the mid-19th century the answer to that is more than likely a resounding – Yes!

Nearly 3 million men from both the north and south fought in the war. It's been widely accepted that between 600,000 to 660,000 men from both sides died between 1861 and 1865, but new research puts that number higher – maybe as high as 750,000 men that perished during those four years. All these men left their homes, families and all that they knew to fight for their beliefs. With such a large percentage of the population participating in the Civil War it's more than likely one, if not several, of your ancestors fought.

So, where do you begin as you search for your ancestor's place in the tremendous struggle known as the Civil War? It's not as hard as you might think and begins in your own home.

First take a look at your oral family history. Your grandparents or great grandparents may have stories that they were told about their Civil War veteran grandfather. Write those stories down. You'll want them for a variety of reasons, but in your Civil War research you're bound to refer back to these golden tales. Make sure you ask some specific questions like where your ancestor lived. What city, state or territory? Did he serve in the infantry or cavalry? Was he an artillery man or sailor? Was he a private or an officer? Questions prompt memories and those reminisces may produce information you'll find valuable.

Many families have an oral history that was written down by the family historian a couple decades ago. I'm thankful someone in my own family hand wrote lineage and bits of information at a 1943 reunion. Though I found some of the information was ultimately incorrect; it was a great starting point to begin my research.

Also look in all of those boxes of family papers your parents weren't able to part with when grandma passed and are stored haphazardly in the attic or basement. You never know what clues you'll find there among obituaries, cemetery deeds and old birth certificates. If you're extremely lucky maybe there's a photo of great grandpa tucked away somewhere too.

If the previous options of checking with elder family members isn't available to you look through your family tree at the generation of men born in the 1830's and 1840's. For me, that generation was great-great grandfathers and there were eight of them. It doesn't hurt to be flexible with dates either. My own Civil War ancestor was born in 1826 and was a whopping 38 years old when he served. So expanding your search to the men in your family who were born in the 1820's is also a good idea. Remember many youths lied about their age and served when only 16 or 17 years old so give those late 1840 births a close look. We all know a little flexibility with data is a plus in genealogy research!

One last thought as you search your family tree for Civil War veterans is to visit the cemetery. Veterans were proud of their service during the war and with honor displayed their company and regiment on their tombstones. Many also received the easily recognizable marble markers with the shield on the front provided by the government. Also look for the cast iron GAR (Grand Army of the Republic, see Chapter Eight) markers stuck in the ground close to a headstone. All are clues to Civil War service. A leisurely walk through the cemetery where your ancestors are buried may produce the information about Civil War service you're looking for.

Marion Township Cemetery, Henry County ,Ohio.   *Photo provided by author*

Rockport Cemetery, Allen County, Ohio.   *Photo provided by author*

You Have A Couple of Names; Now What Do You Do?

Armed with a name or two and perhaps some of your own oral family history try finding your potential soldier in the National Park's Civil War Soldiers and Sailors System at http://www.itd.nps.gov/. Maintained by the National Parks System, their goal with this database is to have documented every person who served in the Civil War. Soldier, sailor, marine, cutter guard, officers, privates, Union, Confederate this site has done well to be as comprehensive as possible.

If you hit a snag and your ancestor's name doesn't show up or there are six men listed with the same name take another look at where he was living in the 1860s. A check of the 1860 United States Federal Census will help you with this. My oral family history had my Civil War ancestor serving from Ohio when in fact he served with a Pennsylvania regiment, which is where the 1860 Federal Census showed the family living. Some questions or brick walls may be broken down when examining oral information a little more closely. Always valuable and a great starting point, oral family history can have its flaws as it's retold through the years. As a genealogist your job is to prove or disprove these facts.

While at the National Park's Civil War Soldiers and Sailors System be sure to click on the Tools page and Info page. There's a lot of great information available and many details on regiments and battles. Being familiar with the battles your ancestor fought, the places his regiment traveled through will help you further your research. Knowing your Civil War veteran's regiment never fought outside the state of Virginia or spent their entire service in the Western theater will help as you sift through information.

Next take your possible Civil War ancestor to the Family Search website. This free site, sponsored by The Church of Jesus Christ of Latter-day Saints (Mormons), has millions of historical records for you to search. You can search by typing in the name of your ancestor, spouse and his date of birth or you're also able to browse their record collections record by record. Some of the titles include Confederate Navy and Marine Service Records, Service Records of Union Colored Troops and Civil War Soldiers Index. Each set of historical records like those just listed have a detailed information page explaining the collection, how to use it and additional resources for continued research, which is very helpful. Take the time to read the information page before you type in your ancestor's name and hit search. It helps to know what to expect from this record set. I'd also suggest you look around the site. Family Search provides many video demos, a blog, and online courses. All helpful as you research. There's a lot of information on this site and it's all free. So take advantage of it.

Just remember all databases are not complete and never can be. The compilation of these records depend on original accuracy of the record keeper, availability, whether they are legible, etc. So while some databases may not be as complete as others; all are valuable resources for clues in researching your ancestor. They are one more tool in your genealogy tool box.

Subscription Sites

Besides using the valuable free sites like the National Park's Civil War Soldiers and Sailors System and Family Search there are subscription sites available to you as you research your Civil War ancestor. Ancestry is probably the most popular and well-known. With billions of indexed online records you may decide to continue your research on their site. Ancestry has the most comprehensive collection of military records available. Along with photos, newspaper articles and obituaries, the Civil War researcher will find a vast amount of documents to pursue. With titles like U.S. Department of Veterans Affairs BIRLS Death File, 1850-2010 or Civil War Prisoner of War Records there will be many record sets to search and/or browse.

If the cost of membership is prohibitive at this time there is an alternative. Ancestry does provide a Library Edition. Check your local library for availability and access.

Discharge Certificates

A helpful research option I've come across is the Civil War soldier's discharge certificate. Upon completion of service the Union Civil War veteran was required to file his Discharge Certificate with his county courthouse. If you know the county your ancestor was living in immediately after the war there is a chance he filed his discharge papers there. There is always the chance

Union Soldier's Discharge Certificate
Published by Currier & Ives, 1865
Library of Congress: Prints and Photographs
Division (No known restrictions on publication)

he did not (as proven by the many listings on EBay). Check with either the Auditor's office or the Clerk of Courts in the county your veteran called home at the end of the war. Information provided on the certificates include soldier's name, company, regiment, enlistment and discharge dates with locations stated as well.

By now you've probably compiled a nice list. You may have your Civil War ancestor's name, spouse, date of birth, death and regiment he served with. Perhaps you've read a little about the battles the regiment fought but your information is limited. In fact the sum of your ancestor's Civil War experience can be stated in five sentences. You'd like to know a little bit more, right? Who was he? What did he do in the war? How did the Civil War change his life? With a little more research you can add to his story. You want to include the human side of the events he participated in. The idea is to shake the dust off your Civil War ancestor, use the important dates and places in his life and put them in sequence adding up to a real person who participated in one of the greatest history changing events this country has ever seen. So let's do more research.

Chapter Two

National Archives

A strong and incredibly valuable resource when tracing your Civil War ancestor's military service is the National Archives and Records Administration (NARA) at http://www.archives.gov. Our nation's archives house files dating back to the American Revolution. This accumulation of data contains documents linked to the military service of its soldiers, pensions and land grants among other things. These files could be the key to the additional knowledge you seek. The two main sources of information for a Civil War soldier are the Compiled Military Service Record (CMSR) and The Pension Applications and Pension Payment Records. Whether your ancestor is Union or Confederate, volunteer or regular army, their military service is recorded here. Along with infantry this includes Naval service as well as the Marines and Coast Guard.

The Compiled Military Service Record is a file containing muster rolls, pay vouchers, hospital rolls and so on. This is usually a smaller file and denotes whether your soldier was present or not during specified periods of time and can reveal some interesting information. Some of the facts you will learn about your Civil War ancestor through his CMSR file are his rank, unit he served with, his muster in and out dates, some limited biographical information like age, eye and hair color, height and weight. There may also be medical information included. I have found some hospital muster rolls in CMSRs that indicated why the soldier was a patient (typhoid fever, lung disease, etc.) but even if it does not list the illness, the dates of the hospital stay are there. All of this is information that is priceless as you discover who your ancestor was. The Compiled Military Service Record (NATF 86) can be ordered online for thirty dollars or you can download the form and mail it in. You have the choice of receiving hard copies or a cd/ dvd of the file.

Photo provided by author

The other source of information available through the archives is the Pension Applications and Pension Payment Records. I have requested pension files on a few soldiers and received a bonanza of information. I've never been disappointed. These files compiled for each individual Union veteran contain such information as discharge papers, birth records, marriage certificates, eye-witness accounts of battles and injuries, etc. The possible genealogy information contained in a pension file is invaluable.

My Civil War ancestor, George Washington Lowery, fought for several pension increases during the latter part of his life so his file contained 114 pages. The amount of information will vary with each veteran, but my great-great grandfather's file included a couple written descriptions of his injury by his doctors as well as the effects of those wounds which lasted his lifetime. Another bonus in the pension file was a letter written by his brother-in-law stating that he, the brother-in-law, had served in another regiment participating in the same battle that my great-great grandfather was injured in. After the battle the brother-in-law upon checking was told my great-great

Declaration for the Increase of an Invalid Pension

Declaration for Invalid Pension, 13 Nov 1890, George W Lowery (Pvt., Co. A, 81st Pennsylvania Volunteer Infantry, Civil War), Civil War Pension Application soldier's certificate number 133419, Case Files of Approved Pension Applications, 1861-1934; Department of Veterans Affairs, National Archives Record Group 15; National Archives and Records Administration, Washington, D.C.

grandfather hadn't survived. So he wrote a letter to his sister breaking the news of her husband's alleged demise. Imagine my great-great grandmother's shock at learning of her husband's death and even greater shock (and hopefully relief) when she learned he survived after all! The letter on the next page was in my great-great grandfather's pension file. What a wonderful family story that had been lost to history yet I was able to unearth it with some research and his pension file from the National Archives.

Respectable and fully Entitled to credit and who bein
-g duly Sworn by me Declairs that he is the Identical
Philip C Lowe who was a Private in Battery D of the
112 Regament of P.a. Artillery in the war of 1861 and
he was with his said Co & Reg on duty at the Battle
of five forks in Virginia on the 7th day of April 1865
And that he knew George W Lowery Priv in Co a 81 Reg of
P a Vol Infy. and knows that Said George W Lowery.
while in the line of his duty then and there was
wounded by a Musket Ball Strikeing him in the brest
& passing through or nearly through his boddy. that
he did not See Said Lowery that day after he was wounde
-d, but obtained his information from Regamental report
And Survivers who knew him, on the day of the
Battle, that he affiant went to look after Said Lowery
the day after the Battle, and did not Get to See him but
was informed that he (Lowery) was shot through
the brest near the heart and was dead or could not
live but a short time, which inteligence he (affiant)
wrote to his (Lowerys) wife the day after the said
battle, that he (affiant) now lives in Ballville
Township Sandusky Co Ohio and his Post office
adress is Freemont Sandusky Co Ohio and that he has
no interest in George W Lowerys application for a
Pension or in Prosecuting the Same
                                    Philip. C Lowe
            Subscribed in my Presence and Sworn
to before me this 15th day of July 1874 and I
further Certify that the foregoing affidavits were

Phillip C. Lowe,
Affidavit before
Probate Court,
Seneca County
Ohio 15 July,
1874.
(The original
handwritten
affidavit is in the
Civil War Pension
File, George W
Lowery, soldier's
certificate number
133419,
Case Files of
Approved
Pension
Applications,
1861-1934;
Department of
Veterans Affairs,
National
Archives Record
Group 15;
National
Archives and
Records
Administration,
Washington, D.C.

Now if you're wondering whether your Civil War ancestor has a pension file the place to look is the Civil War Pension Index. Found online through any of the major databases like Ancestry, FamilySearch, Fold3 and of course on microfilm at the National Archives, this file is a collection of the nearly 2.5 million applications for pensions based upon service during the Civil War. The cards contain the applicant veteran's name, state and regiment he served with, as well as who filed for the pension if other than the veteran. A pension could be applied for by widow, child or dependent mother.

Rachel H Millikin, Mother's Claim for Pension, 30 April 1864, James R. Van Meter (Pvt., Co. F, 4th Ohio Volunteer Cavalry), Civil War Pension Application soldier's application number 51554, Pension Files of Veterans Who Served Between 1861 and 1900; National Archives Record Group 15; National Archives and Records Administration, Washington, D.C.

The second pension file I requested belonged to my first cousin, four times removed, James Van Meter. He died of disease during the Civil War. At only 21 years of age and having never married or fathered children I thought his story ended at his death. I ran his name through the Civil War Pension Index not expecting any information in return only to find that Rachel Millikin had filed for a pension on behalf of James' military service. Rachel was his mother's name but I wasn't familiar with the surname. When I received James' file it was filled with letter upon letter written by his dependent mother, Rachel Millikin, seeking a pension after James' death. The letters outlined the death of James' father, her remarriage and the drunkenness and neglect of her second husband. How James sent money to her from each pay and how desperate she was after his death. In fact the file included two handwritten letters by James himself to his mother during the Civil War referring to the money he sent home to her. James Van Meter's pension file was a windfall of genealogy information. His story is not lost and all because I happened to check to see if a pension had been filed on behalf of his military service.

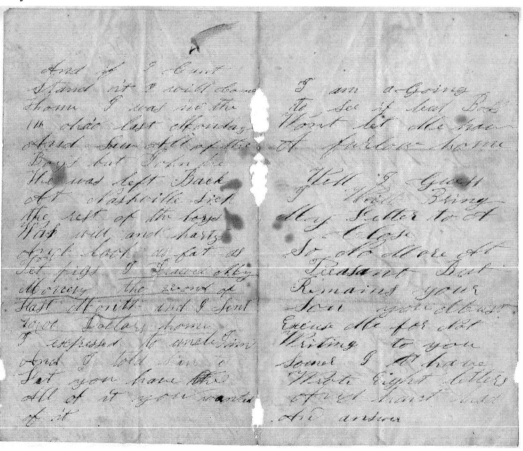

James R. Van Meter, Letter to his mother Rachel H Millikin, 20 October, 1862. The original handwritten letter is in the Civil War Pension File, James R. Van Meter, application number 51554. Pension Files of Veterans Who Served Between 1861 and 1900; National Archives Record Group 15; National Archives and Records Administration, Washington, D.C.

The Pension Applications and Pension Payment Records (NATF Form 85) can be ordered online for eighty dollars or you can download the form and mail it in. You have the choice of receiving hard copies or a cd/dvd for your files.

If your Civil War ancestor was a Confederate soldier the best place to research his service is through the state he served with. If he received a pension it would come from the state level not the federal government. You can contact the appropriate state archives. (See Appendix B) The NARA site has a comprehensive section for your search of Confederate Pension Records through the individual state's archives. http://www.archives.gov/research/alic/reference/state-archives.html Included are addresses, phone numbers, and the state's website. Some states have pension records, lists of enlistment oaths and discharges, even Confederate Home records. This is a good place to start as you research your Confederate Civil War ancestor. Another site you might check is the Council of State Archivists at http://www.statearchivists.org/states.htm. This list with live links includes all 50 states and territories.

To get your research started the State Archives you might contact when searching for your soldier's Confederate Pension or other available information is listed in Appendix B. Not all of these states belonged to the Confederacy but the archives may contain information on your Confederate ancestor like amnesty papers, grave sites or a manuscript collection. A complete list of all State Archives and contact information may be found on the NARA and Council of State Archivists sites mentioned earlier.

A final thought, the National Archives site has many free online documents and photos to browse through. Looking at Civil War era pictures and reading documents of the time period gives the researcher a better understanding of the events our Civil War ancestors lived through.

One last note – Fold3 (http://www.fold3.com/) mentioned earlier in this chapter is a paid subscription website dealing primarily in U.S. military records from the 17th to the 20th century. With Ancestry as its parent company, Fold3 claims more than 400 million documents available for search on its site and is continually adding to that total.

For the Civil War researcher some of their sections of interest may include Civil War Service Records, Pension Index, Widows Pension Files, Confederate Casualty Reports, Confederate Citizens File, etc. Like Ancestry, Fold3 does provide a Library Edition. Check your local library for availability and access.

Chapter Three

Civil War Draft Registration Records

By 1863 it was more than apparent the war between the states would not end quickly. The initial patriotic fervor that swept through both sides was nearly extinguished with the reality of the war's massive death toll and number of wounded. The result was lower enlistment numbers, especially in the north. In order to send reinforcements to bolster Union regiments the Civil War Military Draft Act was passed by Congress and signed into law by Abraham Lincoln in March of 1863. This legislation introduced the first draft in U.S. history. A total of four drafts were implemented from this Act during the remaining two years of the war.

There were two classifications for the men enrolled in the draft. Class I were men age 20-35 and those 36-45, all unmarried. Class II encompassed everyone else. All men from ages 18 – 45 were recorded on the rolls as well as immigrants who had applied for citizenship.

This initial record set is known as the Consolidated Lists of Civil War Draft Registrations. These lists of men who registered for the draft can be found at the National Archives (Record Group 110) as well as on Ancestry's site http:// search.ancestry.com/search/db.aspx?dbid=1666. Some of the information that can be found in these draft records include name, age, class, congressional district, residence, profession, married status, birthplace, former military service and if any – additional remarks.

Provost Marshal Records

With the institution of the draft to answer the demand of additional fighting aged men, the need to create a bureau to manage the program was necessary. In March of 1863 the government set up the Provost Marshal Bureau. Created by the federal government yet run on the state level, a Provost Marshal team was assigned to each congressional district. It was the job of this office to document each man in the district. From these lists potential draftees were selected. The other job of the Provost was to arrest deserters.

As mentioned before there were two classifications for the men enrolled in the draft. All men were recorded on the rolls and then given physicals to determine their ability to fight. Men with disabilities were prevented from service.

Including the above mentioned Consolidated Lists of Civil War Draft Registrations the Provost Marshal office created other records as well. They include Registers of Drafted Men, Recruits, and Substitutes, Medical Registers of Examinations of Recruits and Substitutes, Registers of Medical Examinations Showing Rejections and Exemptions and Descriptive Book of Arrested Deserters.

The Provost Marshal records contain a good bit of information on the individuals recorded, from their residence, physical description and health, to their place of birth, age, marital status and occupation. If your ancestor served there is the date he entered the army, whether he was drafted, enlisted or a substitute, the regiment he served with and where he mustered in. If your ancestor had the means he could have paid a three hundred dollar fee or found a substitute to fight for him. Or there's the other side of that, your ancestor may have been the substitute who he was paid to fight for someone else. All that information is documented in the Provost Marshal's records.

The Registers of Medical Examinations Showing Rejections and Exemptions give detailed accounts as to the reasons a man could not serve.

There are also the records on deserters. This register would contain a deserter's name and rank, the company and regiment he left. Also his residence, occupation, date of birth and physical description.

So with all this information available to research where are the Provost Marshal's records? They are also a part of Record Group 110 held by the National Archives and spread between ten regional offices. Unfortunately these collections are not online so you'll need to locate the office that contains the records you want to search and go to them.

NATIONAL ARCHIVES RECORD CENTERS

Seattle, Washington

Boston, Massachusetts

New York City, New York

Philadelphia, Pennsylvania

Chicago, Illinois

Kansas City, Missouri

Denver, Colorado

Riverside, California

Fort Worth, Texas

Atlanta, Georgia

Map Created by Jennifer Alford

A few things to keep in mind as you start your research are know where your ancestor lived and approximately how old he was in 1863. Checking the 1860 United States Federal Census will help you find that information. Also if your current information is vague and you have access to Ancestry.com try the U.S. Civil War Draft Registrations Records, 1863 – 1865 explained in the first part of this chapter. This index will help you know you are on the right track. I found three of the four great-great grandfathers I'm researching there with their congressional district number in the Draft Registration Records! The fourth one I expect will take a little more intense research but I fully expect to find him. With this information I will research the rest of the Provost Marshal records.

I called the Great Lakes Region where the files I'm interested in are kept. The gentleman I spoke with was very helpful, suggesting before my visit I email my list of names, states and districts so they have the opportunity to review the records, making sure they are stable enough for me to search. He was also kind enough to make sure I knew their hours, parking situation, etc. All helpful information before my visit.

The National Archives at Kansas City also provides an informative PDF on the Provost Marshal records and includes the ten regional branches of the NARA at http://www.archives.gov/dc-metro/know-your-records/genealogy-fair/2011/handouts/civil-war-provost-marshal-records.pdf Another good resource to familiarize yourself with these records.

Chapter Four

Special Enumeration of Union Veterans and Widows

"We are all the product of things we've never seen and people we never met. In fact, if just one little detail had been changed in their lives, we may not even exist!" -Melanie Johnston

Most family historians and researchers are well aware that the 1890 United States Federal Census was destroyed by fire. Yet there is a portion of that census still available to us today. Saved from fiery ruin and an ill-advised decision of a Commerce Department worker is most of the Special Enumeration of Union Veterans and Widows or maybe better known as the 1890 Veterans Schedule.

This additional or "special census" was requested by the U.S. Pension Office. The intent of this supplementary schedule was to help Union Civil War veterans find fellow soldiers to aid them in filing for a pension. A compatriot's affidavit could help verify regiment, service, injury, etc. The plan was to compile the information from this "special census" and place the printed volumes in local libraries for veterans to access. In addition, the supplemental census figures would help the Pension Office in determining the number of yet to be filed claims.

As the Eleventh Census of the United States was recorded a question regarding Civil War service was included on the general population schedule. If the respondent was a Union veteran or widow of a veteran, a notation was made on the general census record and the enumerator pulled out the Veterans Schedule and asked a few more questions.

The information on this Special Enumeration of Union Veterans and Widows can be invaluable. The top part of the schedule lists the veteran soldier's name, rank, regiment, enlistment and muster out dates. I find it interesting that the soldier's length of service is included, such as 1 year, 9 months, 28 days or as in my ancestor's case 10 months, 18 days. Seeing the veteran's length of service written out like that makes the information less abstract and easier to remember.

The bottom part of the schedule includes any additional remarks by the veteran or widow. It could list injury, disability and all sorts of additional information. I've found several notable items from these extra remarks, like a veteran's admission to a soldiers home or, regiment broke up, even deafness, piles or limb amputation.

What's equally important is that enumerators, for the most part, ignored their instructions that only Union veterans were to be recorded. Many Confederate veterans are included in this schedule as well as veterans from other conflicts like the War of 1812 and the Mexican War.

The only disappointment to this great resource is that almost all of the records for Alabama through Kansas and about half of Kentucky are assumed to be destroyed.

Checking the Special Enumeration of Union Veterans and Widows otherwise known as the 1890 Veterans Schedule as you continue your research may add important data to the facts regarding your Civil War ancestor. You can find this census schedule on FamilySearch https://familysearch.org/search/collection/1877095 or on Ancestry http://search.ancestry.com/search/db.aspx?dbid=8667.

The Official Pension Roll of 1883

Another often times unknown and overlooked resource for the Civil War researcher is the Official Pension Roll of 1883. This five volume set lists the names of veteran's receiving pensions at that time. The list contains Civil War veterans and those from the War of 1812. You'll find the name of the person receiving a pension, his assigned pension number, the reason why he's receiving a pension, his post office (city), amount of monthly pension and the date his pension was allowed.

The volumes are organized by state, then by county within the state and then by city. Oddly enough the names are not in alphabetical order so be sure to search your ancestor's city from beginning to end.

LIST OF PENSIONERS.

OHIO—Continued.

HARDIN COUNTY—Continued.

No. of certificate.	Name of pensioner.	Post-office address.	Cause for which pensioned.	Monthly rate.	Date of original allowance.
200, 634	Wolff, John	Kenton	dis. of lungs	$6 00	Jan., 1882
199, 371	Wilt, Jacob	....do	wd. r. shoulder	4 00	Dec., 1881
56, 198	Wetherill, James G.	....do	wd. r. wrist	14 00	....
46, 259	Shawhan, Frederick K.	....do	wd. r. thigh	10 00	....
201, 386	Holmes, Jacob A.	....do	fracture of r. clavicle	2 00	Jan., 1882
49, 699	Strong, Luther M.	....do	wd. l. arm	30 00	....
111, 396	Strong, Wesley A.	....do	wd. in neck	6 00	....
135, 257	Steagall, John W.	....do	wd. r. thigh	2 00	....
193, 846	Herman, Catharine	....do	widow	10 00	Dec., 1881
35, 039	Lewis, Mary Ann	....do	... do	20 00	....
33, 747	McFarland, Eliza	....do	....do	8 00	....
156, 640	Gordon, Catharine A.	....do	....do	8 00	Mar., 1872
8, 846	Murphy, Hannah	....do	....do	8 00	....
188, 113	Watt, Marietta B.	....do	....do	19 00	July, 1880
156, 741	Williams, Mary A.	....do	....do	8 00	Mar., 1872
190, 819	Wilson, Catharine	....do	do	8 00	Jan., 1881

Citation: United States. Pension Bureau (1883). List of Pensioners on the Roll January 1, 1883: Giving the Name of Each Pensioner, the Cause for which Pensioned, the Post-office Address, the Rate of Pension Per Month, and the Date of Original Allowance, as Called for by Senate Resolution of December 8, 1882 3. U.S. Government Printing Office. p. 146. Google Books. Web. 7 Apr 2014

Volume One contains the listings for the New England states, New Jersey and Washington, D.C. Volume Two has the veterans living in New York and Pennsylvania. Volume Three covers Iowa, Ohio and Illinois. Volume Four and Five have the pensioner's from everywhere else.

This is an additional resource to use when researching whether your ancestor was receiving a pension post Civil War. The other source is the Civil War Pension Index was mentioned in Chapter Two. The Official Pension Roll of 1883 was a requirement of the United States Pension Bureau and its compilation was called for by the Senate Resolution of December 8, 1882.

There are two options in researching these records. If you have an account with Ancestry.com you can find their database here. http://search.ancestry.com/search/db.aspx?dbid=31387 Or there is a free version on Google Books (http://books.google.com/books/about/List_of_Pensioners_on_the_Roll_January_1.html?id=prgqAAAAMAAJ) or Archive.org (http://archive.org/details/listpensionerso00buregoog)

The only problem with the free resource is that the outer edges of the pages were not scanned correctly. So some pages you will not be able to get the full last name but I'd check anyway. Maybe the image of your ancestor's page was scanned correctly.

Confederate Amnesty Papers

After the Civil War, President Andrew Johnson made a sweeping amnesty proclamation that would encompass the regular Confederate soldiers, but there were many exclusions to the amnesty declaration that extended to the community. Those excluded from the general amnesty included military officers in the war, governors of Confederate states, senators and congressmen of Confederate states, wealthy landowners and just about anyone who held an office in the Confederacy. This group was required to apply for a pardon and amnesty from the U.S. government.

Those excluded from amnesty were:

1. Diplomatic agents or officials of the Confederacy
2. Persons who left judicial posts under the United States to aid the rebellion
3. Confederate military officers above the rank of Army colonel or Navy lieutenant
4. Members of the U.S. Congress who left to aid in the rebellion
5. Persons who resigned commissions in the U.S. Army or Navy and afterwards aided in the rebellion
6. Persons who treated unlawfully black prisoners of war or their white officers
7. Persons in military or civilian confinement or custody
8. Individuals who had absented themselves from the United States in order to aid the rebellion
9. Graduates of West Point or Annapolis who served as Confederate officers
10. Ex-Confederate governors
11. Persons who left homes in territory under U.S. jurisdiction for purposes of aiding the rebellion
12. Persons who engaged in destruction of commerce on the high seas or in raids from Canada
13. Voluntary participants in the rebellion who had property valued at more than twenty thousand dollars
14. Persons who had broken the oath taken under the provisions of December 8, 1863

If your Confederate Civil War ancestor would happen to fit any of these categories there is a strong probability he applied for amnesty, but remember the average soldier was given amnesty and did not need to apply for it.

Those who did apply for amnesty generated a file. Each individual's file can include paperwork such as a letter asking for amnesty, an oath of allegiance, and letters of recommendation from friends or relatives.

The Confederate Amnesty Papers are online but currently only on the subscription sites Ancestry and Fold3. The Ancestry record set is called the Confederate Applications for Presidential Pardons 1865 – 1867. Fold3's are titled Confederate Amnesty Papers. If you do not subscribe to either of these sites remember to check your local library for availability of the Ancestry and Fold3 free library edition.

Part of the National Archives Record Group 94 this collection has about 14,000 records. They are filed alphabetically by state, then by surname. The average file is a few pages long and usually handwritten.

I was doing some research on two Confederate Civil War veterans that are distant cousins. I was trying to establish parentage when in my research I came across the amnesty papers of David Van Meter, of Hardy County, West Virginia. His packet of papers included a letter of request to President Johnson for amnesty. The letter included his age, 80 years old, where he lived, Hardy County WV, that he had never traveled further than 10 miles from his home and that was to visit his aged, infirmed sister. The letter also stated that he suffered great loss of personal property during the war and was no longer covered under "Exception 13". This letter of application is signed by David Van Meter. There is also a letter of recommendation by two local citizens, David Van Meter's signed oath of allegiance to the U.S. and a letter from the Provost Marshal verifying the information.

In particular the handwritten statements by David Van Meter gave a lot of insight on 1860s life, how he lived, how he ran his farm and several of his encounters with the Union army.

It's certainly worth the effort to research these records for additional genealogy information about your Civil War soldier and his family. You might note your ancestor's neighbors in the 1860 census and check to see if they have a file in the amnesty records. Your ancestor or family may have written a letter of recommendation for the neighbor providing you with a hidden genealogy find.

Chapter Five

Researching Regiments

Up to this point your genealogy research has focused on your Civil War ancestor himself. You've gathered a great deal of data, primarily facts and dates. Now let's look at your veteran as part of the "whole" researching his movements in the army in which he served.

One of the first pieces of information discovered about your Civil War ancestor was probably the regiment he served with. You've also been able to find the company he belonged to as well. This information is almost as important as your soldier's name. Along with his dates of service, his company and regiment help identify locations, battles and his experiences.

Most Civil War soldiers enlisted in a regiment raised in the area in which he lived. The majority did not travel far to volunteer and joined locally with relatives, neighbors and friends. This is a good point to remember when looking through a regimental or company roster. Just as a genealogist looks for the movements of an extended family group from one location to another the Civil War researcher should look for brothers, brothers-in-law, cousins and neighbors in the same regiment.

An infantry regiment was made up of ten companies, each company with one hundred men. Your ancestor lived, ate and fought with those 100 men. Even if your ancestor did not leave a journal or letters describing his experiences reading and familiarizing yourself with his regiment and the documents they left behind will provide insight into the experiences of your veteran. As mentioned in Chapter One, knowing the origins of your ancestor's unit as well as being familiar with the battles he fought will help you understand his Civil War life and aid in evaluating future information.

Keep an eye out for information regarding your ancestor's company movements. As you've read my great-great grandfather served with Co. A 81st Pennsylvania Volunteer

Infantry. I'm always alert to Company A's orders especially if they were assigned to a duty separate from the entire regiment.

Going a step further make a little cheat sheet on the structure of the army in which your ancestor served. Use it as a bookmark so it's always handy as you read. Especially in the early days of extended reading on regimental histories, corps movements and battles fought it'll help keep clear in your mind your ancestor's troop movements. Keeping corps and brigades with their commanding officers straight makes it easier to comprehend where your ancestor fit in. You'll also be able to easily locate the text pertaining to your ancestor in sources like the Official Records which is covered in the next chapter.

You may have to update your cheat sheet as you find commanding officers are replaced or regiments are combined with others, but soon you'll find you've read enough to recognize names, brigades, etc. and you'll know whether the source you are researching applies to your ancestor's unit. **Appendix C** has my suggestion on a cheat sheet.

Since you've established the regiment your soldier served with it's time to read where and how he served. One of the first places to look for a regimental history is at the Civil War Archive, http://www.civilwararchive.com/RESEARCH1/reghistory.htm Their list of histories are linked to Google books where you will be able to download the history in a .pdf format to your computer. Ideal to read and refer back to often.

- Another source is the U.S. Civil War Regimental Histories in the Library of Congress at http://www.loc.gov/rr/main/uscivilwar/ The Library of Congress link also lists letters, diaries, unit rosters, reunions, and other materials for particular regiments.

- Ancestry has a regiment search page - http://search.ancestry.com/search/db.aspx?dbid=3866

- The National Parks Service has a regimental search page at http://www.nps.gov/civilwar/search-regiments.htm

- The Ohio State University has an online Confederate Regimental History with links for each state as well as the Confederate States Army, Divisions and Corps. http://ehistory.osu.edu/uscw/features/regimental/kjones/confeds.cfm

Even a general search of the regiment you are interested in on Amazon or your favorite search engine will provide options in obtaining published unit histories for further reading.

As mentioned earlier even if your ancestor didn't leave a journal or letters describing his war experiences, soldiers within his regiment/company did. Check university manuscript collections, libraries and newspapers. Some of these resources are digitized and online if not check and see the institution's policy on reviewing items in their collection. There may be limitations on handling documents due to fragility and so on.

In researching the history and movements of the company and regiment your Civil War ancestor belonged to you will have a better understanding and appreciation for his service and his sacrifice.

County Histories, Regimental Rosters and other Reading

Along with reading regimental histories there are numerous other options to choose from as you attempt to learn more about Civil War era life. While at the library or on Google Books look for the county history where your Civil War ancestor lived. Many county histories were written for a centennial celebration and included short biographical sketches of the county's outstanding citizens. Most were written in the late 1800's and the bios mention the Civil War service of the men included in the history.

The National Park's Service Civil War Soldiers and Sailors database is the most complete roster of Civil War soldiers and sailors in entirety, but there are others. After the war most individual states published a Regimental Roster listing the regiments raised in the state and the men who served. Many rosters needed several volumes for a complete account. Listed numerically by regiment and then alphabetically by soldier surname the roster gives age, residence and a few brief remarks about his service such as killed in action, January 1, 1864 re-enlist, transferred to 32nd Infantry and so on. There might be a clue to further research in your own ancestor's listing. Most libraries still have a set of their state's regimental roster but rosters are easily accessed online as well. A typical search engine query will produce a digitized copy of a state's roster for research through the state archives, Google Books, etc.

Any library has shelves and shelves of Civil War books ranging from specific battles, to a soldier's life or women spies. The more you familiarize yourself with the events and attitudes of the 19th century you're better able to understand documentation, customs, words and phrases peculiar to the time.

Again I'll suggest that you take a look at the manuscripts department of universities and colleges. Many have extensive collections of family papers, diaries and journals that pertain to the Civil War or life at that time. In many cases descendants that lived across the country from where their Civil War ancestor lived inherited family papers and donated them to the educational institution near their current home. I've seen Pennsylvania regimental information in California repositories. Think outside the box as you investigate all potential resources.

Chapter Six

The War of the Rebellion: a Compilation of the Official Records of the Union and Confederate Armies

"It is a desirable thing to be well-descended, but the glory belongs to our ancestors." -- Plutarch

This well-known source is used by Civil War enthusiasts as they study troop movements and officer's decisions yet it's a little used resource in the genealogy research of Civil War ancestors. *The War of the Rebellion: a Compilation of the Official Records of the Union and Confederate Armies* does sound overwhelming to wade through but stay with me for a minute. Otherwise known as the Official Records or OR for short, these 128 volumes are a collection of actual reports, orders and correspondence of those who fought in the Civil War. This collection includes records from both the Union and Confederate armies. There isn't a similar source for the "other side"; both armies' military information has been compiled in the Official Records. Now I know it's hard to get past the title. It spells b-o-r-i-n-g! Then add to that the knowledge it's written by army and navy officers says you're in for dull, dry reading ahead. Let me tell you though it doesn't have to be that way.

Let's put aside our original "ugh" thought and do an online search of *The War of the Rebellion: a Compilation of the Official Records of the Union and Confederate Armies*. There are a few places online that have digitized this information. Cornell University is one http://ebooks.library.cornell.edu/m/moawar/waro.html and The Ohio State University is another http://ehistory.osu.edu/osu/sources/records/, place where this work may be viewed online. You can also find the set in many libraries if you'd like to read from an actual book. Even my smaller local public library as well as my local museum's library has this set of books.

In using the Official Records as a resource I'm going to refer to the Cornell University web page. They have an easy to use site that explains how the Official Records are searched on their site. The Official Records are compiled according to the campaign, either in the eastern or western theater and then in chronological order. Usually the Union report is first, then followed by the Confederate report.

Next is the list of each volume with the explanations of contents. In my search I was interested in the actions of Co. G, 9th Ohio Volunteer Cavalry (OVC) on April 13, 1864. A corporal I'm researching died on that date outside of Florence, Alabama. So I scrolled down until I found:

> Volume XXXII – in Three Parts. 1891. (Vol. 32, Chap. 44)
>
> Chapter XLIV – Operations in Kentucky, Southwest Virginia, Tennessee, Mississippi, Alabama, and North Georgia. January 1-April 30, 1864.
>
> Part I – Reports
>
> Part II – Union and Confederate Correspondence, etc.
>
> Part III – Union and Confederate Correspondence, etc.

I click on reports and find myself immersed in the actions of both Union and Confederate regiments. Then I come across this:

> . . . . *On the night of the 12th instant detachments of the Twenty-seventh Alabama and my regiment, commanded by Colonel Jackson and myself, crossed the Tennessee near Tuscumbia and surprised a camp of the enemy 4 miles distant from the river, killing 3, capturing 3 commissioned officers, 38 noncommissioned officers and privates, and 1 negro sutler, together with a considerable number of horses, mules, arms, equipments, comprising the larger portion of Company G, Ninth Ohio Cavalry. I brought off my detachment entire, sustaining no loss whatever. One-half the prisoners I took charge of, and have this day forwarded them to Tuscaloosa with a guard of 1 captain and 14 men, to be turned over to the provost-marshal of that district. . . (1)*

This actual narrative describes what happened to Co. G, 9th Ohio Cavalry on that day in April 1864 as reported by Col. Samuel S. Ives of the 35th Alabama. I can't find a corresponding Union report so I click on Union and Confederate Correspondence to find Union Brigadier-General G. M. Dodge write:

> *. . . Colonel Rowett reports heavy force on opposite side of river, but thinks that they have as yet only crossed in squads. They captured one company of Ninth Ohio Cavalry yesterday morning before daylight, and got them across without firing a shot. This is the first expedition of that regiment. They are evidently green. All sorts of rumors down in that country. Rowett says they are building boats at Prides, 12 miles below Tuscumbia, and hauling them to six different points on the river. The rest of the Ninth Ohio Cavalry is with Rowett before this, and he will watch close . . . (2)*

This passage was the Union's response to Co. G, 9th Ohio Volunteer Cavalry (OVC) being taken prisoner by the 27th & 35th Alabama regiments. The information put a new light on what I already knew about the corporal and the 9th OVC. Most of Co. G was taken prisoner without firing a single shot, they were newbies on the battlefield and it showed. The Union corporal I was researching was one of the three who died.

The information found in the Official Records is written by the soldiers and/or officers who witnessed the events. These reports give the researcher a first-hand account of the experiences their Civil War ancestor lived through. Without your ancestor's personal letters or a diary this is as close as a researcher may get to witnessing the events your Civil War veteran experienced.

This research example pertained to a very small skirmish. Imagine how numerous the reports and messages will be when researching a major battle or extended campaign. Following a timeline of the battles your ancestor participated in and researching each one through the Official Records will give the researcher a very clear picture of the hardships, weariness and actual fighting experienced by nearly every Civil War soldier. I recommend researching *The War of the Rebellion: a Compilation of the Official Records of the Union and Confederate Armies* for a more complete picture of your Civil War veteran.

(1) Source: United States. War Dept., The War of the Rebellion: a Compilation of the Official Records of the Union and Confederate Armies, Govt. Print. Off., 1880 – 1901, Series 1, Volume 32, Chapter 64, pg. 355, online digital collection Cornell University.

(2) Source: United States. War Dept., The War of the Rebellion: a Compilation of the Official Records of the Union and Confederate Armies, Govt. Print. Off., 1880 – 1901, Series 1, Volume 32, Chapter 64, pg. 663, online digital collection Cornell University.

Chapter Seven

Confederate Military History

As researchers strive to round out the persona of their Civil War veteran there are a number of resources available. Databases with facts and dates, all kinds of literature, some publications are even written by those who fought. They are the "Official version" of the records written by the men who experienced the events. These selections were gathered, edited and published a century ago, yet available to the researcher today. The accounts by the soldiers themselves tell us so much. We can feel the struggle today just as they experienced it.

The Confederate Military History is one of those records. I've found it to be another good reference as I do Civil War research. Along the same lines as the *Southern Historical Papers* explained later in this chapter or the *Official Records of the Union and Confederate Armies* in the preceding chapter, the *Confederate Military History* gives us a first-hand account of the war from those fighting for the Confederacy.

Photo provided by author

The Confederate Military History, published in 1899 includes 12 volumes edited by Clement A. Evans who wrote two of the volumes himself. Evans had vast first-hand experience in the war. Born and raised in Georgia he organized a company called the Bartow Guards who eventually joined the 31ˢᵗ Georgia Infantry and became Company E. Evans led troops through such battles as Gettysburg, the Wilderness and Spotsylvania. Evans was wounded a couple times during the war yet always came back to lead his troops. Such bravery and tenacity led to promotions and Evans was a brigadier general by the end of the war.

In 1895 Clement Evans published the *Military History of Georgia* which made him the obvious choice to oversee the compilation and editing of the *Confederate Military History*. The twelve volumes include:

> Volume I – Secession and Civil History of the Confederate States
> Volume II – Maryland and West Virginia
> Volume III – Virginia
> Volume IV – North Carolina
> Volume V – South Carolina
> Volume VI – Georgia
> Volume VII – Alabama and Mississippi
> Volume VIII – Tennessee
> Volume IX – Kentucky and Missouri
> Volume X – Louisiana and Arkansas
> Volume XI – Texas and Florida
> Volume XII – Military and Post War History

In researching Co. B 11ᵗʰ Virginia Cavalry which was raised in Hardy County, (West) Virginia. I chose Volume 2 and read:

> "This repulse was soon afterward converted into a route by Col. Lomax's regiment, the 11th Virginia Cavalry, which now took the road with drawn sabers, and charged down the turnpike under a fearful fire of artillery. Without this attack it is certain that our trains would have fallen into the hands of the enemy."(1)

I found the text easy to read and not as dry as some military accounts. I also found some interesting tidbits, like Co. E spent some months defending their own hometown and county seat. It was fascinating and powerful reading especially from that point of view.

If your Civil War ancestor fought for the Confederacy, the *Confederate Military History* is a great resource to document his troops movements and activities during the war. Written by those who were there, you'll feel the events as well as read them.

If your Civil War ancestor fought for the Union choose the volume in the state he fought in. All volumes are well indexed and the chapters are divided by year. You can easily skip to 1863 if that's when your ancestor was in the service. Reading how the Unions armies battled Confederate regiments in the *Confederate Military History* gives you a broader view of the fighting in which your ancestor participated.

The best part is that the *Confederate Military History* is easily accessible online. I found it through The Internet Archive Text Archive at archive.org through the Allen County Public Library (Ft. Wayne, Indiana). Here's a link to get you started. http://archive.org/details/confederatemilit02evan

The Southern Historical Society Papers

Similar to the Official Records or *The War of the Rebellion: a Compilation of the Official Records of the Union and Confederate Armies,* the Southern Historical Society Papers are first-hand accounts of Confederate regiment activities in the Civil War.

The Southern Historical Society Papers was the brain child of General Dabney Maury. As an ex-Confederate officer, Maury wanted the southern side of Civil War history documented. So he, along with other notable Confederate officers like P.G.T. Beauregard and Braxton Bragg, came together to collect and preserve southern records and battlefield accounts.

As these, and other society members, representing all southern states gathered information, the amount of written material grew to the point of establishing a library, which was located in Richmond. Their members continued to gather material such as southern military reports and casualty lists. Letters and diaries were collected, officer's recollections and transcripts from the Confederate Congress recorded. Some of the military reports accumulated were so detailed they were later copied right into the Official Records of the War of the Rebellion by the United States War Department.

In the early days of compiling records the society published them as articles in newspapers and magazines. As the amount of information grew the society made the move to a book format and the first volume of the *Southern Historical Society Papers* was released in 1876. A total of 52 volumes were published over an 82 year period.

The Southern Historical Society no longer exists today but most of their records were turned over to the Museum of the Confederacy. You can check their website at http://www.moc.org/ regarding their archives. The great thing about today's technology is that we can access a lot of that information online. Just go to Tufts University http://www.perseus.tufts.edu/hopper/text?doc=Perseus:text:2001.05.0001 or Google Books http://bit.ly/1cpXhEX to find many of the volumes of The Southern Historical Society Papers online.

An example of what's available, in Volume 35 of the Table of Contents you'll find the 11th Virginia at the Fight of Five Forks, or Roll of Co. A, 7th Virginia Cavalry and the 11th Kentucky Cavalry.

Clicking on Roll of Co. A, 7th Virginia Cavalry, I get a more detailed title Roll of Co. A, 7th Regiment Virginia Cavalry Rosser's Brigade. Listed alphabetically are the men of Co. A with details as to where they live in 1906, who was wounded in the war, and which soldiers had passed on since the war. Nice genealogy information here.

I was interested in the week of April 1-7, 1865. My great-great grandfather, George Washington Lowery, was a Union private with the 81st Pennsylvania and part of the Second Corps pursuing Lee and the Army of Northern Virginia west across the state. Here's just a little I found regarding the Battle of Sailor's Creek on April 6th, 1865 . . .

> *"There was no time for deliberation. He immediately marched the battalion by the right flank obliquely to the rear, fixing bayonets as they went, so as to face this unexpected enemy, and, reforming his line, attacked at once with the bayonet, while they were yet entangled in the wood. The (Savannah) Guards were but eight-five that day, and nothing but the disorder of the enemy in the thicket saved them. . . . (2)*

Then on April 7, 1865 at the Battle of Cumberland Church where my great-great grandfather was wounded it reads . . .

> *"On Friday, April 7, 1865, Farmville, Va., was reached, and Scales' brigade relieved Cook's brigade as rear guard of the infantry. The enemy having crossed the river, pressed the lines very hard and consequently the rear guard was engaged in several attacks and suffered severely. The enemy was driven off, and this was the last fighting in which the regiment (38th North Carolina) was engaged before surrender . . . . (3)*

These are the actual words of men who fought those battles. They looked across the battlefield where my great-great grandfather's regiment was entrenched. There's much to be learned about our Civil War veterans' experiences in these pages of the southern accounts of the war.

If your Civil War ancestor fought for the Confederacy, *The Southern Historical Society Papers* is a worthwhile resource in documenting his regiment's service in the war. If your Civil War ancestor fought with Union forces take a battle he participated in and research the Confederate regiments in that same battle. Checking those Confederate regiments or dates of battle in *The Southern Historical Society Papers* will give you another view of the fighting your ancestor was engaged in.

(1) Evans Clement, A., Confederate Military History, Atlanta, 1892, Volume 2, Page 82, Allen County Public Library (Ft. Wayne, IN) online digital collection.

(2) Brock R. A., Southern Historical Society Papers, Richmond, 1895, Series 1 Volume 23, Page 253, Google Books online digital collection.

(3) Brock R. A., Southern Historical Society Papers, Richmond, 1897, Series 1 Volume 25, Page 263, Google Books online digital collection.

Chapter Eight

Researching "Old Soldiers Homes"

Another lesser known resource when researching military ancestors is the U.S. National Home for Disabled Volunteer Soldiers or commonly referred to as the "Old Soldiers Home".

The homes were established for Civil War veterans who had been injured during the war and found they or their families could no longer care for them. The homes were established across the country and veterans were able to voluntarily check themselves in and out. Your veteran may have lived close enough in proximity to have stayed at a home for a while.

The locations of these homes, referred to as Branches, included Togus Springs, Maine known as the Eastern branch. The Northwestern branch Home for Disabled Volunteer Soldiers was in Wood, Wisconsin. The Central branch was in Dayton, Ohio. The Southern branch was built in Hampton, Virginia and the Western branch, considering the time in which it was built was in Leavenworth, Kansas.

Of course as veteran's medical needs increased so did the number of "Old Soldier's Homes". Additional branches were built in Sawtelle, California and it was known as the Pacific branch. Illinois was the location of the Danville Branch and Indiana had the Marion Branch. In South Dakota the Battle Mountain Sanitarium was built in Hot Springs. New York had the Bath Branch and the northwest part of the U.S. saw the Roseburg Branch constructed in Oregon. Several homes sprung up in the south. Tennessee was the home of the Mountain Branch in Johnson City. There was the Tuskegee Home located in Alabama, a Florida branch in St. Petersburg and Mississippi had the Biloxi Home.

Home for Disabled Volunteer Soldiers, Sandusky Ohio   *Photo provided by author*

Records were kept on each veteran who checked in and those registers are now kept at the National Archives in Record Group 15, in the Records of the Veterans Administration. The National Archives has a very informative page on the history of the Homes for Disabled Soldiers at http://1.usa.gov/L3BtR2, but they do not have the records online. They are available for research on FamilySearch https://familysearch.org/search/collection/1916230 and Ancestry http://search.ancestry.com/search/db.aspx?dbid=1200

When searching either website you'll be able to view a copy of the actual record. I have found most records to be well-filled out with valuable information. Some of the items contained in an individuals' record includes name, rank, company, regiment, discharge, date admitted to home, birthplace, age, religion, residence, marital status, name and address of nearest relative, pension information, date and cause of death and place of burial (if applicable). The bottom of each veteran's page has a space for general comments as well. I have even found height, hair color, eye color and complexion included on one record.

If your Civil War veteran fought for the Confederacy he may have stayed at a state-run Soldiers Home. In that event, contact the state archives in the state where the home was located. A list of state-run homes can be found on the National Archives website as well at http://1.usa.gov/JZgsam

Using this resource adds another dimension to your military ancestor. His injury and need for health care makes him real and helps us tell his life story more completely.

Roll of Honor: Soldiers Interred in National Cemeteries

A lesser known resource is the *Roll of Honor: Names of Soldiers Who Died in Defense of the American Union, Interred in National Cemeteries*. This is a 27 volume set that was originally published in 1866 and updated in 1994.

More than 270,000 Union soldiers are listed in the Roll of Honor. There is a complete index to this work to help locate a soldier's name. You'll find a section for soldiers who died on the battlefield and a section for those soldiers who died of disease or wounds in hospitals or as a prisoner of war in a Confederate prison.

The origins of this work are rooted in the Mexican War. Fought from 1846 to 1848 approximately 1,733 U.S. soldiers died. Most of their bodies were never recovered and are buried in Mexico City. Very few of these men were ever identified.

To prevent this from happening again the War Department issued General Order #75, dated September 11, 1861. The order states that the commanding officers of military departments and corps were responsible for identifying and burial of dead soldiers.

To help with this process President Lincoln signed an act ten months later that enabled the purchase of ground for National Cemeteries. Twelve National Cemeteries were established in 1862 and the job of burying the Union dead during the Civil War fell to the Quartermaster Department.

In many case those soldiers who died in battle were buried close to where they fell. Some of those graves were well marked but most were not. Often great numbers were buried in a mass grave or in trenches. One example of this is at Spotsylvania Court House. There were thousands upon thousands of casualties on both sides from this battle. Only a few of the bodies were buried shortly after. A year later when those dispatched by the Quartermaster Department went back to bury the Union dead only 700 were identified. Thousands became "unknown".

After the war, in 1866 the Quartermaster's Department gathered their records to publish where fallen Union soldiers were buried and reinterred. It was found that most of the records were sloppy. Many names were misspelled and the handwriting was illegible. Some bodies that were reinterred were not recorded and of course there were those unidentifiable. The volumes came out haphazardly as a book here and another published months later. The attempt to never again have U.S. soldiers unidentified and their resting place unknown fell short. Yet there is still a lot of information on thousands of Union soldiers. Twenty-seven volumes to be exact.

The 1994 edition of Roll of Honor is an updated, comprehensive list of the final resting place of Civil War Union soldiers who died on the battlefield. It is as complete as is possible.

As you research you will find the original place of interment for your soldier, his name, rank, company, regiment, date of death, second interment with cemetery section and grave number. If you have questions as to where your Union Civil War ancestor is buried your answers may be in these volumes.

I searched WorldCat.org and found the 1994 set available at most university libraries in my area. The 1860's edition is online at Archive http://bit.ly/19f4lVo. If possible I'd search the newer work.

The name of this selection again?

Roll of Honor: Names of Soldiers Who Died in Defense of the American Union, Interred in National Cemeteries. United States Army, Quartermaster Dept. Baltimore, MD: Genealogical Publishing Company 1994

Chapter Nine

Grand Army of the Republic

You live as long as you are remembered. -- Russian proverb

The Grand Army of the Republic (GAR) was an organization comprised of honorably discharged Union Civil War veterans who had fought in the U.S. Army, Navy and Marines. The group was founded in 1866 initially to support veterans and their families as well as being a means for veterans to keep in touch with their comrades after the war. Yet as their numbers grew so did their power and political clout. By the 1890s membership was close to half a million men and the GAR's influence helped elect notable Republican Union Civil War veterans like U.S. Grant, Rutherford B. Hayes and James Garfield to the U.S. presidency.

More important than its political power the GAR worked to secure federal pensions for veterans, they established soldiers' homes and did other relief work for the benefit of their membership. They promoted patriotism participating in parades and wreath laying ceremonies to honor fallen veterans. In fact it was the GAR's National Commander-In-Chief General John Logan who established the first Decoration Day, or Memorial Day as we now know it. A day set aside to honor the Civil War's fallen Union soldiers by placing wreaths and flowers on their graves.

GAR members met locally and that group was referred to as a post. Most small towns and villages had a post with larger metropolitan areas having more than one. Ohio alone had 745 organizations. Posts were named after Civil War soldiers who had passed on, many times honoring a soldier who had died in battle. The local posts belonged to their state "Department", such as the Ohio Department or Iowa Department, and both the posts and departments fell under the umbrella of the national organization.

The national and departments held yearly conventions or "encampments". The encampments generally spanned several days and included business meetings, memorial services, dinners, fellowship as well as "camping out."

GAR membership was an important part of a veteran's life. Through this very powerful group a former soldier was cared for both physically and emotionally as he socialized with other soldiers who had similar war experiences.

Photo provided by author

A veteran who wanted to join his local post was required to fill out an application for membership. This would include his current vital information as well as his military experience. Once accepted the new member's information was logged in a Post Descriptive Book. Some posts even had a Memorial Book. Each member had a page in the Memorial Book where personal background information was recorded and even his memories of his military service. The information might include mentions of the veteran's friends in his regiment and his obituary after his death. Of course there would be Minute Books in each post which would include lots of names and information regarding the activities of the post.

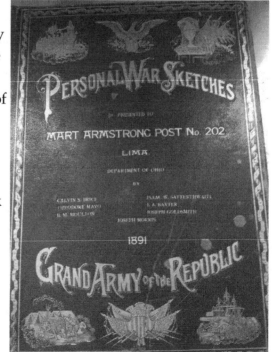

I found the Memorial Book for one of the local GAR posts in my hometown museum. Called Personal War Sketches this huge, oversized book was engraved for Mart Armstrong Post No. 202. Inside were beautifully illustrated pages where members in their own hand wrote where and when they were born and enlisted. What battles they fought in, how and where they were

Photo provided by author

46

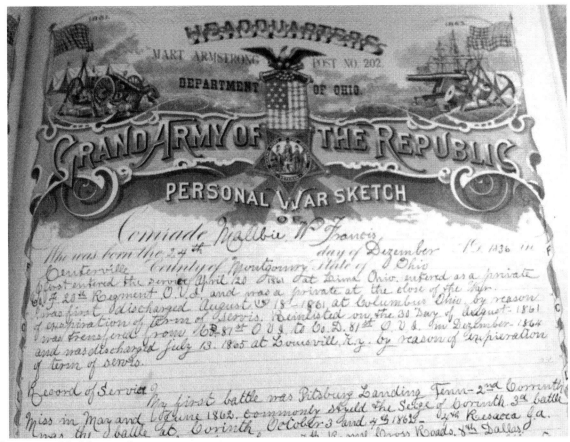

Photo provided by author

injured, even at which hospital they recovered. Some sketches included names of friends they fought alongside or a particular event they chose to remember. This book is a goldmine of information and written in the member's own hand.

Of course as Union veterans died so did the strength and numbers of the GAR. The last member passed away in 1956 and the GAR no longer existed. The records and minutes of individual posts were many times donated to local museums, libraries and historical societies. By now you can see the records of a GAR Post would be very helpful as you research your Civil War ancestor.

- A few places to research the GAR is at this Library of Congress page. It lists posts by locale and state. http://www.loc.gov/rr/main/gar/

- The Grand Army of the Republic Library and Museum is located in Philadelphia and its holdings contain the records of many posts nationwide. http://garmuslib.org/

- The Sons of Union Veterans are compiling a list of GAR documents and where they are located at http://www.garrecords.org/

- FamilySearch.org has a few GAR links on their site https://www.familysearch.org/learn/wiki/en/Union_Veterans%27_and_Lineage_Society_Records#The_Grand_Army_of_the_Republic_.28GAR.29.

- Ancestry also has a couple links for Kansas GAR posts.

- If you live in the area, the New England Civil War Museum might be an excellent place to research. Their library originated with GAR Burpee Post 71. This GAR post started its own reading room and library for the members and has now grown in to the New England Civil War Museum. http://www.newenglandcivilwarmuseum.com/libraryarchives.htm

- Wisconsin Veterans Museum has a substantial GAR collection at http://wisvetsmuseum.com/about/history/

- There's also the GAR and Civil War Museum in Marblehead, MA. http://www.marbleheadmuseum.org/GARMuseum.htm

- At Google Books you'll find the - Records of Members of the Grand Army of the Republic: With a Complete Account of the Twentieth National Encampment ... A History of the Growth, Usefulness, and Important Events of The Grand Army of the Republic, from Its Origin to the Present Time. (http://books.google.com/books/about/Records_of_Members_of_the_Grand_Army_of.html?id=0WOAAAAAIAAJ)

Most importantly try your local museums, libraries, universities and historical societies to see if they have a GAR collection. My own museum's library has a GAR collection for another area town as well as the War Sketches Book for the post in my city but none of this was readily accessible. I would never have known it existed if I hadn't inquired about possible GAR records at my museum.

United Confederate Veterans

Soon after the Civil War there were many local veterans groups spread across the south. These veteran groups met to renew old friendships, document their battle history, remember those who had gone before and lend a helping hand if needed. It wasn't until 1889 that all the smaller groups came together to become the United Confederate Veterans (UCV). Officially organized in New Orleans the UCV became the national group for Confederate veterans.

The United Confederate Veterans membership was open to all former soldiers and sailors who fought honorably for the Confederacy. The aim of the organization was to record an impartial history of the events of the war, to help the disabled veteran, the needy, to care for widows and orphans as a result of war, to honor and remember all who had died in battle and to preserve the friendships forged during the harrowing events of battle.

Photo provided by author

As was the post-war custom for most veteran's groups the UCV was set up in a military style. The local groups were known as "camps". The Camps were numbered and named. The Camps belonged to a Division (State), Divisions came under a Department. Originally there were three Departments named for the Army of Northern Virginia, Army of Tennessee and Trans-Mississippi. Finally all fell under the National organization. At its peak there were 1,885 camps in the UCV with a membership of 160,000.

The National organization held a yearly reunion in major cities across the south. Starting as a one day event reunions eventually grew to three days of meetings and fellowship for veterans, widows and children of deceased soldiers. The final United Confederate Veterans reunion was held in Norfolk, Virginia in 1951.

During the height of its membership the UCV published the Confederate Veteran magazine. It came out monthly from 1893 until 1932. This is a valuable genealogy resource. The magazine was filled with articles as veterans retold their war time experiences. Names, obituaries, pictures and descriptions of events filled the pages. It's a treasure trove for a genealogist researching their Civil War ancestor.

As with any organization the United Confederate Veterans kept records. These records would be quite helpful researching your Civil War ancestor. Camps generated rosters, minutes from meetings, new member applications, etc. as well as all the information recorded on the Division, Department and National level.

The United Confederate Veterans was an important part of a veteran's life. Not only was he able to honor and remember his fallen comrades, help their families, he was reunited with remaining veterans and able to renew the special bonds of brotherhood forged during his war years.

So now you can see the records of the UCV would be a great asset as you research your Civil War ancestor. Thankfully there are many web sites to search.

- First try the Sons of Confederate Veterans site here—http://sonsofconfederateveterans.blogspot.com/2011/01/records-of-united-confederate-veterans.html They list the known repositories of larger collections of UCV records.

- Then there is a vast amount of UCV information at Archive.org. http://archive.org/search.php?query=creator%3A%22United+Confederate+Veterans%22 Listed are names of Departments, Divisions, Brigades and Camps, their commanders, etc.

- Familysearch.org has films in their Family History Library for the United Confederate Veterans Association. https://familysearch.org/learn/wiki/en/Confederate_Veterans_and_Lineage_Society_Records The records are listed according to state and camp. There are rosters which of course include names, company or rank, regiment, state and name and location of the camp.

- If you type in United Confederate Veterans records in your search bar numerous individual state records sites will be listed. There are also sites that include actual programs and rosters of individual reunions with PDFs you can download. All valuable reading as you understand your post war ancestor's life.

- Also try the resources available through the *Confederate Veteran Magazine*. First go to the Library of Virginia site here: http://lva1.hosted.exlibrisgroup.com/F/?func=file&file_name=find-b-clas65&local_base=CLAS65 You'll be able to search all issues of the magazine for a reference to your veteran ancestor. Not only will you get the volume and page of the magazine that references him you could also get other helpful information. I typed in David Van Meter and got his birth date and place, death date and place, regiment served with, as well as the magazine issue he is listed in.

- I can check that issue at the University of Pennsylvania's Online Books page. http://onlinebooks.library.upenn.edu/webbin/serial?id=confedvet Here I clicked on Volume 29 page 186 to see the reference of David Van Meter. This site is missing the magazines from 1924 through 1930.

- Familysearch.org is another possibility to research all issues of the *Confederate Veteran Magazine*. https://www.familysearch.org/learn/wiki/en/Index_to_the_Confederate_Veteran_Magazine,_1893-1932 Check their Family History Library Catalog for the films of interest to you.

As a side note there is a current publication titled, *Confederate Veteran Magazine* published by the Sons of Confederate Veterans (SCV). It has current events and information for today's SCV members and is not a Civil War genealogy resource.

Chapter Ten

Southern Claims Commission

"The story of his great-grandfather . . . was his own story, too." -- *Kelly Cherry*

The Southern Claims Commission was a program set up by the U.S. government during the Grant administration. It was in effect from 1871 to 1880. The aim of this commission was to reimburse southern citizens who were pro-union or Union loyalists for their property lost during the war. This loss could range from a store owner or farmer whose goods or property was seized to aid the Union Army, to the homeowner who was displaced when their residence was used as a field headquarters.

The claims were allowed in the southern states of Alabama, Arkansas, Florida, Georgia, Louisiana, Mississippi, North Carolina, South Carolina, Tennessee, Texas, Virginia and also West Virginia.

The commission was comprised of a three member panel set up to review the claims submitted by loyal Union southern citizens who had suffered a loss during the war. In total more than 22,000 claims were submitted to the commission with a mere 7,000 approved for any type of reimbursement.

So why research such a database? Because each claim made, whether allowed or disallowed is packed with genealogical information. Applicants had to provide a substantial amount of information to back up their claim that they were Union loyalists, had property loss while aiding the Union army and did not help the Confederates in any manner. Each file is very similar to a pension file with name, age and residence. There are physical descriptions, family members listed, local military engagements described and so much more. Applicants first had to prove their loyalty to the Union and then prove their property loss. This was done by answering an extensive list of questions as well as providing the testimony of neighbors to verify their claim.

The accounts given by neighbors reveal real civilian life during the war and perhaps interaction with your ancestor. Where many Civil War resources are compiled reports given by officers during the war, the documents contained in the Southern Claims Commission files are first-hand accounts of everyday people and how they dealt with war-time life. Maybe your ancestor's daily life.

Let's take for example the file of William Randolph of Hardy County, West Virginia. Contained in this file are several handwritten letters by Mr. Randolph explaining his Union allegiance among neighbors who were Confederates. Two of Randolph's neighbors Thomas Maslin and S. H. Alexander also wrote letters verifying Randolph's loyalty claim. In fact both describe how Randolph's home sat between the enemy armies and William had to traverse between the two camps as he farmed. One letter states the area was overrun by McVeil's Rebel Rangers. Interesting stuff and some real insight into William Randolph's life.

Items listed in the file as confiscated from William Randolph included:

1863	Seven horses - $910
	64 Tons Hay - $960
	25?? Flour - $175
	91 Bushel Corn - $72.80
Spring 1864	Two Workhorses - $300
Fall 1864	Two horses - $230
Feb 1865	Three horses - $430

(1)

Depositions in the file verifying this property claim are from William Randolph, H.G. Maslin, S.H. Alexander and J.W. Duffey. Here's a small excerpt:

Moorefield, August 28, 1879

Samuel H Alexander being duly sworn deposes and says as follows:

My age is 43, residence here, occupation at present keeping the Mullins Hotel. I was born and raised here, and have known W. Randolph over twenty years. His wife is first cousin to my wife. During the war I was in the Confederate army. I had the impression from the very beginning, & felt satisfied that Mr. Randolph took the union side, all the way through. In the spring of 1863 I first met him at Harrisonburg where he was placed under my charge as a prisoner. The only charge I heard against him was that he was a Union man and carrying news to the Federals. He was discharged without a trial so far as I recollect. . . . His reputation was that of a Union man. I so regarded him and felt like censuring him for it, and that was the feeling towards him among the Confederate soldiers who knew him . . . . (2)

This particular file held more than 100 pages and provided a wealth of information on William Randolph, Samuel Alexander and the others who came forward on Randolph's behalf. I can't emphasize enough the volume of genealogical information contained in this file.

Some of the standard questions and answers asked of both claimant and witnesses when a case was opened can be found in the files. Such as:

5. On which side were your sympathies during the war and were they on the same side from beginning to end?

6. Did you ever do anything or say anything against the Union cause and if so what did you do or say and why?

44. After the presidential election of 1860 if of age, did you vote for any candidate or on any questions during the war and how did you vote? Did you vote for or against candidates favoring secession? Did you vote for or against the ratification of the ordinance of secession or for or against separation in your state?

66. Who was the owner of the property charged in this claim when it was taken and how did such person become our owner?

68. Has the person who owned the property when taken since filed a petition in bankruptcy, or been declared bankrupt?

Maybe the most significant portion of these files is that previous slaves also filed claims as well as testified on behalf of applicants. In these statements made by previous slaves rich genealogy information can be found.

70. Were you a slave or free at the beginning of the war? If ever a slave when did you become free? What business did you follow after obtaining your freedom? Did you own this property before or after you became free? When did you get it? How did you become owner and from whom did you obtain it? Where did you get the means to pay for it? What was the name and residence of your master and is he still living? Is he a witness for you and if not why not?

71. Were you formerly the slave of the claimant? Are you now in his service or employment? Do you live on his land? Are you in his debt? Are you in any way to share in this claim if allowed?

This documented information given by previous slaves may be one of the few resources for researching African-Americans during this era.

Whether your ancestors were Union or Confederate as long as they lived in the above named southern states there is a chance you'll find them in these files. Browse the records of the county in which they lived. Your family may not have made a claim but they may have filed an affidavit for a neighbor who did.

Where are the Southern Claims Commission records? The entire set of records has three parts, the Index, Allowed Claims and Disallowed Claims. You will find all three at Ancestry http://search.ancestry.com/search/db.aspx?dbid=1216 (this link is for the index) and Fold3 http://www.fold3.com/title_12/southern_claims_commission/ which of course are subscription sites but you can access this at libraries with the Ancestry Library Edition.

Other helpful resource pages on the Southern Claims Commission can be found at FamilySearch (https://www.familysearch.org/learn/wiki/en/
Southern_Claims_Commission), the National Archives (http://www.archives.gov/
legislative/guide/house/chapter-06-war-claims.html) and (Dick) Eastman's Online Genealogy Newsletter (http://blog.eogn.com/eastmans_online_genealogy/2007/03/

southern_claims.html).

Confederate Disability Applications

As researchers tracking down our Civil War ancestors we're finding they left us quite a paper trail to follow. Even after 150 years with a little perseverance we can follow that trail and get a more complete picture of who our ancestor was and how he lived. Here's one more step on that path, using a really interesting site, as we continue to investigate the lives of our ancestors who fought in the Civil War.

The Confederate Disability Applications Database is located on the Library of Virginia's site. This database contains the applications of Virginia Civil War veterans who sought help purchasing artificial limbs and other disability benefits after the war.

Available between 1867 and 1894 the Virginia General Assembly passed a measure which would help those Civil War veterans in medical need. They set up a Board of Commissioners on Artificial Limbs for this purpose and veterans applied for assistance whether it was for artificial limbs or other disability help. Applicants had to submit quite a bit of documentation to receive aid. This information included where they lived, what unit they served with, where they served and how they were injured. Veterans stated what help they were seeking and included their medical history after their injury. They submitted as much information as possible to receive the assistance requested. Very similar to a pension file, all this information is available on the database. I found most soldier's files had at least six documents.

This legislation was passed by the Virginia General Assembly. So of course it was open only to the residents of Virginia but there were applicants who served with a Virginia regiment and lived elsewhere either during the war or after when they applied for assistance. I encourage you to check the database even though you know your Civil War ancestor lived in another state after the war. Many applicants were turned down for assistance but the documentation they provided is still available on the site.

Chickamauga and Chattanooga National Military Park   *Photo provided by author*

One little quirk I found as I searched the files was that all the documents are saved as tiffs which makes them a little harder to read when you open them. I just saved the documents to my desktop and opened them from there for much easier reading and printing. If I found I didn't need that particular document it was easy enough to throw away.

Reading a few of these files helped me to see the impact of war and war injuries on veterans. Whether Billy Yank or Johnny Reb, the war forever changed the lives of veterans, especially those with injuries. My Civil War great-great grandfather didn't lose a limb, but was shot in the chest. The lingering effects of that injury played a major role in his health the rest of his life.

So check out the Confederate Disability Applications Database which is on the Library of Virginia's website. It's valuable genealogy information on our Civil War ancestors.

(1) Source: The National Archives and Records Administration. Southern Claims Commission Approved Claims, 1871-1880: West Virginia, Record Group 217, Publication Number M1762, Roll 0001, Claim Number 54968, pg. 2, online digital collection Fold3

(2) Source: The National Archives and Records Administration. Southern Claims

Commission Approved Claims, 1871-1880: West Virginia, Record Group 217, Publication Number M1762, Roll 0001, Claim Number 54968, pg. 29, online digital collection Fold3

Chapter Eleven

African American Civil War Soldiers

The Emancipation Proclamation issued by President Abraham Lincoln on January 1, 1863 paved the way for the enlistment of freed slaves and free African American men to serve in the Union Army during the Civil War. By May of that year the Bureau of Colored Troops was established and all newly formed regiments of African Americans were now recognized under the heading the United States Colored Troops (USCT).

There were African American regiments formed before this time like the renowned 54th Massachusetts and the Native Guards and Corps d'Afrique of Louisiana but now the door was opened for a greater number to serve.

Nearly 180,000 African American men mustered into infantry, cavalry and artillery regiments of the Union north from 1863 to 1865. Sadly nearly one third of that number perished during the war.

In the south both free and enslaved African Americans fought for the Confederacy. In late 1863 slave owners could enlist their slaves for military service and receive three hundred dollars. Many took advantage of this but it is agreed the number of African Americans who fought for the south was much smaller and with a lack of accurate records makes even approximate numbers unknown.

So are the research methods much different when trying to find your African American Civil War ancestor? Not exactly. The formula outlined in Chapter One as well as the rest of the book applies here.

First review your family tree taking a look at the generation of males born anywhere from the 1810's to the late 1840's. These men in their late teens, twenties and thirties are more apt to be involved in military service during the Civil War.

Review your family's oral history as well. Were stories of battles or war time souvenirs handed down through the generations?

Are there any documents stored in your parents or grandparents attic or basement? Be sure to look for obituaries which may list military service. Asking these questions of elder family members is a good place to start.

Remember to visit the cemetery. A majority of veterans' tombstones are engraved with their company and regiment. They may

Photo provided by author

also have the government marble markers with the shield on the front. Look around for a cast iron GAR (Grand Army of the Republic, see Chapter Eight) marker stuck in the ground close to a headstone. All are clues to Civil War service. A walk through the cemetery not only improves your health it may provide clues toward the information you're looking for.

Check the 1860 United States Federal Census for age and residence.

As mentioned in Chapter One, researching your veteran at the National Park's Civil War Soldiers and Sailors System (http://www.itd.nps.gov/) Choose U.S. Colored Troops in the state column. This check will help clarify his actual service and the regiment he served under.

The National Archives and Records Administration (NARA), as mentioned in Chapter Two, is this country's "family attic". Historical records dating back to this country's inception have been preserved there and are available for research.

The Compiled Military Service Records (CMSR) of Volunteer Union Soldiers Who Served with the United States Colored Troops is the individual soldier's various records assembled into one file. This includes his information from contain documents such as muster rolls, enlistment papers, correspondence, orders, casualty reports, descriptive rolls, hospital rolls and pay rolls to create compiled military service records. Of course additional information included in these files are name of soldier, his age, place of birth, enlistment date and location and in many instances there is additional information which came from the descriptive rolls, like injury, illnesses, etc. This is Record Group 94 and the information is from microfilm M1801, M1817-M1824, M1898, and M1992.

Fold3 has the complete United States Colored Troops (USCT) Service Records found here: http://www.fold3.com/title_681/civil_war_soldiers_union_colored_troops/ In a joint partnership between the National Archives and Fold3 close to four million documents with detailed information on former slaves was digitized and is available on the Fold3 site. Completed in the spring of 2013 the USCT military service records are readily available for research. If you do not have a Fold3 subscription these files can also be seen free of charge on computers at the National Archives research facilities.

You can access U.S. Colored Troops Military Service Records, 1861 – 1865 on the Ancestry website at http://search.ancestry.com/search/db.aspx?dbid=1107

Family Search also has the record group United States, Service Records of Union Soldiers Who Served in the United States Colored Troops that can be found here https://familysearch.org/search/collection/1932431

Check the Civil War Pension Index then request Pension Applications and Pension Payment Records. These files compiled for each individual veteran contain such information as discharge papers, birth records, marriage certificates, eye-witness accounts of battles and injuries, etc. It is possible the genealogy information contained in a pension file could be invaluable in your research. In many instances the veteran had to fight for his pension or increases thereafter which resulted in excessive amount of paperwork. Much work for them is a gold mine of information for the researcher today.

Also check Provost Marshal records (see Chapter Three). A Provost Marshal team was assigned to each congressional district. It was the job of this office to document *all* men in the district.

The Southern Claims Commission as noted in the previous chapter is another potential resource.

I have found a couple of blogs I think will add a great deal more insight to the research of your African American Civil War veteran.

- The USCT Chronicle "Telling African American Civil War Stories, of Soldiers, Civilians, Contrabands, First Days of Freedom, and the Events that led to Freedom" at http://usctchronicle.blogspot.com/

- The Black Confederate Soldiers at http://www.blackconfederatesoldiers.com/

- A3 Genealogy blog has a great deal of information on African Americans and the Civil War (http://blog.a3genealogy.com/search/label/African%20American)

- The Ancestor Hunt has a detailed section on African American Online Historical Newspapers at http://www.theancestorhunt.com/1/post/2013/10/african-american-online-historical-newspapers-summary.html#.Uml-nyQRVuS

African American regiments when given the opportunity played a vital role in the Civil War. Using the suggestions in this book will enable the researcher to trace their ancestor's service and follow their footsteps.

Chapter Twelve

Regular Army Civil War Ancestor

Was your Civil War ancestor Regular Army and not one of the vast number of volunteers that answered President Lincoln's call for troops? If so, you've probably found him difficult to research. There's more information available on the volunteer soldier than the Regular U.S. Army soldier, yet there are still sites available to help you in your research.

At the start of the Civil War in April 1861 much of the U.S. Army had been deployed west. Most units were sent to fight Indians and protect the settlers on the frontier. When war broke out back east most Regular Army units were brought back to the states to fight. With a majority of Regular Army units fighting in the eastern theater, Regular Army comprised less than 5 percent of the Union troops in the Civil War.

Even so it was the Regular Army Generals that were in charge of the volunteer army. Much has been written about Regular Army generals. History has made many famous, some infamous, but let's see what we can find out about the Regular Army Soldier.

The first place to search for any Civil War soldier is the Civil War Soldiers and Sailors database maintained by the National Park Service. http://www.nps.gov/civilwar/ soldiers-and-sailors-database.htm This listing includes 6.3 million names as well as regiment information, battle descriptions, Medal of Honor recipients, prisoner of war lists, cemeteries and so on. This is your starting point. While on the site you might look at some of the other information the National Park System provides. It's very helpful in understanding this timeframe in our country's history.

Gettysburg National Military Park   *Photo provided by author*

Once you have a unit try Family Search. Maintained by the Church of Jesus Christ of Latter-day Saints, this site has volumes of information and continuously adds to their databases. A couple links to check out in your research:

United States Registers of Enlistments in the U.S. Army, 1798 - 1914
https://familysearch.org/search/collection/1880762
Here you will find records of those who enlisted in the regular U.S. Army during the Civil War. Many records are incredibly detailed and can include the date a soldier enlisted, where and by whom. The entries also detail the period of time the soldier enlisted, his city, state, occupation and age. Some even have physical descriptions like height, weight, color of eyes, hair and complexion. There is also date of birth and county and miscellaneous remarks. Those miscellaneous remarks have great information like: Died of wounds in action July 2, 1863 at Gettysburg Pennsylvania, or Discharged Sept. 14/64, by expiration of service, at Little Rock, Ark. This may be the best online research link available for Regular Army personnel in the Civil War.

United States Civil War Widows and Other Dependents Pension Files, 1861-1934
https://familysearch.org/search/collection/1922519
This set of records will give you the veteran's name, the person applying for pension's name, the relationship if not the veteran, veteran's birth date or age and place, his military unit and company and the application number. The first FamilySearch link above will allow you to see the actual image of the document, this second link only provides the information. You will need a paid Fold3 subscription to view the image

of the document but you can get the transcribed information on FamilySearch. Another research stop can be Ancestry.com with these links to pursue.

U.S. Army, Register of Enlistments, 1798-1914
http://search.ancestry.com/search/db.aspx?dbid=1198

U.S. Returns from Regular Army Regiments, 1821-1916
http://search.ancestry.com/search/db.aspx?dbid=1198 and http://search.ancestry.com/search/db.aspx?dbid=1225

U.S. Returns from Military Posts, 1806-1916
http://search.ancestry.com/search/db.aspx?dbid=1571
These records date from the early 1806 to 1916. Here you will find information like the units serving at a particular military post, names of officers and records detailing events at the post. This is an excellent database but you will need an Ancestry.com paid account to research on this site.

At Google Books there is a great resource if your ancestor was an officer. *Historical Register and Dictionary of the United States Army, from Its Organization, September 29, 1789, to March 2, 1903* Volumes 1 & 2 by Francis B. Heitman. (http://bit.ly/19VA6Ch) Lots of information here between the two volumes and can be researched on Google Books free of charge. You'll find information on Regular Army officers and officers in the volunteer army as well. This includes descriptive information for each officer's military service, like rank, the state where he was born, if different than the state where he was originally appointed from and there's information about commissions. There's also lists of battles for the Regular Army and casualty reports.

Another valuable avenue in the research of your Regular Army Civil War veteran is the National Archives. http://www.archives.gov/research/military/genealogy.html There you can obtain a copy of your veteran's Pension Claim file. This file does have a cost as outlined in Chapter Two, but the information you might possibly receive may very well off set the price. A pension file contains the application for pension as well as supporting information like marriage certificate, discharge papers, witness depositions, letters, descriptions of events during service, etc. I have found mountains of previously unknown information in pension files. Search the National Archives website. As mentioned earlier a pension file can be ordered online or by mail.

Although fewer in number than the state militia volunteers, the regular U.S. Army soldier was essential in the ongoing War Between the States. A little extra research effort is needed but that perseverance will be rewarded with helpful genealogical information that will shed light on the man your U.S. army soldier ancestor was.

Chapter Thirteen

Newspapers

Newspapers may be one of the last resources you have on your Civil War ancestor check list. In fact as a family historian you may shy away from newspapers. Genealogists are well aware that newspapers, although chock full of history including names and dates can be tedious to research. Many historical newspapers are still not indexed so the researcher needs to select an approximate date and physically scan page after page for any information or a reference to information regarding their ancestor.

Please don't let this put you off from researching your Civil War ancestor via newspapers. There is so much to learn about this turbulent era of our country's history by reading the articles, ads and editorials of the day. Reading historical newspapers really puts you in your ancestor's shoes. It's almost like a form of time travel.

Start off by checking the local newspapers from your Civil War veteran's hometown or locale during the war. The search will produce articles about the regiments that were raised in the area as well as citing soldiers by name. These articles may list battles fought, some in extensive detail, naming those injured, killed or missing from the regiment.

Many times soldiers themselves wrote home about their own personal experiences and that of the regiment. The local papers would print those letters in their entirety. There were two newspapers in my hometown during the Civil War. Captain Mart Armstrong, Co. B 81st Ohio Volunteer Infantry wrote a weekly letter home that was printed by both newspapers. From training drills in camp to actual combat the folks at home were kept apprised of their hometown heroes' military life.

The political fervor of your Civil War ancestor's home is also revealed in era newspapers. I just assumed that since I live in the Yankee north this area was a big backer of President Lincoln's reelection in 1864. Reading newspaper articles from that time I find this area had a good many "Peace Democrat" or "Copperhead" residents that were very vocal during the presidential campaign.

Along with articles and letters about the regiment's movements, hometown papers also have snippets about daily life and how the residents were doing their part to support their boys in the war. Some of these columns are just as interesting and important as reading about the soldiers themselves.

Gleaning all this information from historical newspapers helps the researcher better understand your Civil War ancestor, the climate of the times he lived in and perhaps his view on the events unfolding around him.

So where do you look for access to historical newspapers? The first section of sites I have listed below contain a variety of newspapers available online. Although there are some small town papers most listed are for cities with a larger population. A few of these websites are:

- Chronicling America is a partnership between the Library of Congress and the National Endowment for the Humanities. This is an ongoing project of gathering and compiling newspapers from 1690 to the present. This is the search link for the newspapers currently digitized. http://chroniclingamerica.loc.gov/search/titles/

- Penn Libraries of the University of Pennsylvania Libraries has a detailed list of online newspapers. This link http://guides.library.upenn.edu/ historicalnewspapersonline is not just for the state of Pennsylvania, but lists all states whose papers are available for research.

- The Online Historical Newspapers blog site also has a wealth of information as well as tutorials for online newspaper searches. http:// onlinehistoricalnewspapers.blogspot.com/

- Free Newspaper Archives – Check out their link for Small Town Papers. Some papers are archived for only a few years and recent years for that matter, but a few do go back as far as 1865. A quick check will let you know if the papers you're interested in are available. http://www.xooxleanswers.com/free-newspaper-archives/us-state-and-local-newspaper-archives/

Also if you scroll down on this same page further below the Small Town Newspapers you'll also get a list of U.S. newspapers by state.

Some sites exclusive to Civil War newspapers available for online research include:

- Virginia Tech – American Civil War newspapers https://dcr.emd.vt.edu/vital/access/manager/Index?site_name=American%20Civil%20War%20Newspapers

- Penn State – Pennsylvania Civil War era Newspaper Collection http://digitalnewspapers.libraries.psu.edu/Default/Skins/civilwar/Client.asp?skin=civilwar&AppName=2&AW=1382378907961

- Son of the South – Harper's Weekly *the* newspaper during the Civil War http://sonofthesouth.net/leefoundation/the-civil-war.htm Reading Harper's Weekly will give you a great overview of the war written at the time.

Besides these free online websites there are paid subscription sites for historical online newspaper research. A few include Ancestry, Newspaper Archive, Fold3, ProQuest and Genealogy Bank. Each individual site boasts millions if not billions of newspaper pages to search. Also remember to check your local library to see if they have a free edition of some of these sites enabling you to research through their library services.

One thing to always remember is that only a small and I mean small percentage of genealogical information is online. The bulk of the records, documents and newspapers that would help in your research are sitting in repositories across the country. So once you've exhausted the resources listed above consider exploring other outside sources.

Start by checking university collections. In my area for example Bowling Green State University (BGSU) in Bowling Green, Ohio houses the Center for Archival Collections (CAC). The CAC has a newspaper collection encompassing 19 counties of northwest Ohio. They have more than 650 titles microfilmed. There are loads of historical newspaper reading there.

Don't neglect smaller universities as well. The University of Bluffton (OH) much closer to me than BGSU has a smaller collection yet they have microfilm of the Bluffton News which I'm interested in reading. Of course you'll need to take your search on campus if you find a university that has microfilmed newspapers of interest. Just be sure to check the On Campus Guide for Researchers so you'll know what's available to the public, their hours and parking information before making the trip.

Finally be sure to check the public library in the area your Civil War ancestor lived. To my surprise the small public library in my town has microfilmed both newspapers that published in the past with dates back to 1843. I would never have imagined such a collection existed in my own backyard. Be sure to ask about this availability in the reference department.

Newspapers may be one of the last resources you have on your Civil War ancestor's research list but don't hesitate long. Search and experience the life your ancestor lived as you read from the newspapers he read.

Chapter Fourteen

Civil War Headstones

As I mentioned in the first chapter your family cemetery is a great place to continue your research into your Civil War veteran's life. Veterans were proud of their service during the war and with distinction displayed their company and regiment on their tombstones. Others received the easily recognizable marble markers with the shield on the front provided by the government. I will add here there is a noticeable difference between Union and Confederate white, marble headstones. One quick look will answer the question as to which side the deceased belonged. Union headstones have a rounded top while the tops of Confederate headstones come to a point. These marble markers were not the only headstones provided to veterans by the government. Veterans were also able to choose a flat marble or granite marker. They were rectangular in shape and approximately 24 inches long and 12 inches wide and had the same limited inscriptions of the upright marble markers.

Photo provided by author

"Government issued headstones" pre-date the Civil War. It was back in this country's frontier days when military posts were built that a burial system was established. As is common due to sickness, injury or combat, soldiers died where they were stationed and post commanders needed to bury them. A cemetery section was set aside usually within the fort for these burials and a marker was placed on each grave. Those markers soon became standard across all military posts — a wooden board with a rounded top and a name or inscription on it.

Woodlawn Cemetery, Lima, Ohio   *Photo provided by author*

This worked fine until the Civil War. With the astounding number of battlefield deaths a more detailed and organized system was needed. Commanders were still in charge of burying their dead but now would be helped out by the Quartermaster of the Army who was to supply wooden headboards and blank books to record soldiers' burials. With the frequent large numbers of burials during the war federally run national cemeteries were born.

By 1873 it was realized the wooden grave markers in national cemeteries would need to be replaced often which would result in a tremendous ongoing expense. So a more permanent solution like a stone monument was needed. That's how the recognizable white marble slab with the rounded top and added sunken shield on the face came to be used.

Now to the good part. By 1879 veterans buried in private cemeteries could obtain the same headstone supplied to those buried in national cemeteries. We know many veterans did acquire them. We see those headstones in the cemeteries we visit today.

Those headstones lead us to a paper trail. An application needed to be filed for a headstone, which resulted in a bunch of records and a database for us to search today.

Known as the United States, Applications for Headstones for Military Veterans this record set is located in the National Archives and is known as Record Group 92. There are two groups in the set. The first set of applications covers 1925 to 1941. Don't be thrown off by the years covered here. Civil War veterans' applications are in this group. Many headstones were applied for by family members long after their veteran died. The second set of applications are from 1941 to 1949. Both record sets are available to research.

The applications contain a lot of information if your ancestors sought a military headstone for their Civil War veteran. Some of the details you may find include the name of the soldier or sailor, his rank, company, regiment and state, the date of his death, religious symbol if used, the name of cemetery with city and state where the veteran is buried and the name and address of the person making the application. Finally the name and address to whom the headstone was being shipped. This can be some very useful information with new leads and surprises.

FamilySearch provides a great resource page for searching the Applications for Military Veterans. Their information page is here: https://familysearch.org/learn/wiki/ en/United_States,_Applications_for_Headstones_for_U.S._Military_Veterans_% 28FamilySearch_Historical_Records%29 The page to actually search the collection from 1925 to 1941 on FamilySearch is here: https://familysearch.org/search/ collection/1916249

Ancestry also provides the information on their site as well. Their records cover 1925 to 1963. http://search.ancestry.com/search/DB.aspx?dbid=2375

Pillars Application for Military Headstone from FamilySearch (1)

This image is from the Joseph H. Pillars application for a headstone. Although not an ancestor, I "met" Joseph when researching the local GAR post in my area earlier in the year. I found it interesting that the GAR post commander is the one who applied for Joseph's headstone. Another new insight is that there's also an address listed for Joseph Pillars on the application. Further research could be done in the City Directory. One of the best parts of genealogy research is finding information that fills a gap within your family files or clues that lead to bigger and better finds.

One last note, the overwhelming majority of these records will be for veterans who fought for the United States. That also includes other military actions like the American Revolution, War of 1812 and the Spanish American war but there are a few Confederate records as well. In 1906 Congress approved headstones for Confederate soldiers that were buried in federal cemeteries. Those headstones were chiefly for prisoners of war who died in Union prisons or Union hospitals. In 1929 Congress extended the availability of headstones for all Confederate soldiers buried in private cemeteries too.

Who knows what helpful bits of information you may glean from checking the United States, Applications for Headstones for Military Veterans. It's another resource as you continue to research and detail the life of your Civil War ancestor.

Find A Grave

Find A Grave at http://www.findagrave.com/ is an online web site where contributors upload photographs of grave sites and their locations making them available for anyone to view without charge. Started in 1995 the founder wanted to expand his hobby of discovering famous people's graves and share them virtually with those who were interested. The site has continued to grow as thousands have added graves of ancestors as well as entire cemeteries. Find A Grave can be a bonus to family historians or genealogists searching for a grave site across the state, across the country or across the world.

You can search this database by name or cemetery. Once you find an ancestor or upload one to the site the viewer also has the ability to leave flowers or a note on the memorial page.

If you don't know where your Civil War ancestor is buried a quick search in Find A Grave may prove beneficial. There is always the chance your ancestor's final resting place has not been documented on Find A Grave. If this is the case you'll want to add him when located and the rest of your family to the site as well.

Billion Graves (http://billiongraves.com/) is a similar site encouraging participants to take photos of headstones with their smart phones recording the GPS location so that headstone can be easily found by anyone throughout the world. Billion Graves has their own app for both IPhone and Android operating systems.

Billion Graves names reflects their goal of recording a billion graves before many are lost to time and the elements. You can search this database by name or cemetery too. Also try searching for your Civil War ancestor on the Billion Graves site. Both are ideal in attempting to locate a headstone unknown to your family.

(1) "United States, Applications for Headstones for Military Veterans, 1925-1941," index and images, *FamilySearch* (https://familysearch.org/pal:/MM9.1.1/VHZ6-NRK : accessed 05 Aug 2013), Joseph H Pillars, 1926.

Epilogue

Now that you've read and used the tips provided here in researching your Civil War ancestor you've got quite a bit of information. Not only do you have names and dates you have facts and experiences.

Congratulations! Your persistent research has paid off. Your Civil War ancestor is more than a name on a regimental roster. You've followed his footsteps and put together information to reveal a life lived with quite a bit of adventure and daring. Don't leave that valiant life resting in the accumulated pages of a binder or electronically preserved on your laptop for your eyes only. Shake the dust off your Civil War ancestor with a storyline, a narrative, a short biography of your veteran's life.

Your first thought may be that you're not a writer but let's look at this a little closer. As a descendant and family historian, you are the one that can link your ancestor's Civil War military service to the 21st century. You can make your ancestor come alive to your children and grandchildren. You do this by chronicling his place in history. As a tribute, compile the service and experiences of your soldier using the facts you've learned so far from your research. Long or short, descriptive or succinct make sure your Civil War ancestor doesn't slip back into the pages of history.

An example of this is what I've written about George Washington Lowery, my great-great grandfather.

> "George Washington Lowery was drafted July 19, 1864 at Chambersburg, Pennsylvania. He was assigned to Co. A, 81st Pennsylvania Volunteer Infantry for three years. Born in Franklin County, PA he was a 37-year-old laborer. At 5 feet 9 inches tall, with a fair complexion, grey eyes, and dark hair, he was an average guy, his description not uncommon for the time.
>
> Serving during the latter part of the war he was a draftee. I suspect my grandfather left his wife and six children a bit reluctantly to answer the call of his country.
>
> After a brief two-month training stint to make the "every-day man" a soldier, Lowery and the rest of the recently drafted recruits were sent to join their regiment. The 81st

Pennsylvania had been mired with the rest of the Second Corps at Petersburg, Virginia, which had been under siege for months. Even though they were in the midst of war, it has been written that many Confederate officers who lived in the area were able to slip away and visit with family and attend Sunday church services. The fighting here didn't come in intense bursts as so many other battlefields but it was long, hard months of exhaustive trench warfare.

Soon my great-great grandfather was about to learn the true magnitude of war. His regiment pulled out of Petersburg and was involved in what is now known as Lee's Retreat. The pursuit of Gen. Robert E. Lee and the Army of Northern Virginia, west across the state, in the final week of the war. The experiences this regiment endured would hardened any soldier. This was the time George experienced the full impact of fighting. The nine months dug in at Petersburg probably did not prepare him for sleeping only moments at a time, the constant skirmishes and out-right battles. His regiment continually moving, marching with the weight of supplies and a rifle. Smoke so heavy in the air an infantryman couldn't see where his bullet hit if it hit anything at all. The regiment found sporadic food consumption a luxury. Yet above all that – experiencing those you'd come to depend on, your fellow soldiers, your friends, ripped apart by flying shrapnel. The thud of a minie-ball as it plunges into a human body. The yelling, cursing, and then slow moans as the injured soon become casualties. It was during this time my great-great grandfather came to know the full meaning of war.

There was the fighting at White Oak Road, where the Confederates prevailed. The battle at Sutherland Station was a union triumph due in great part to the fighting of the 81st. The battle at Sailor's Creek was some of the bloodiest fighting of the war, yet recognition has been lost to the surrender at Appomattox, which was only three days away. There was the skirmish at High Bridge, reminiscent of a modern day movie, and finally just outside Farmville, on April 7, 1865, was the Battle of Cumberland Church, where George Washington Lowery was wounded. As the 81st Pennsylvania, 2nd NYHA and part of the 5th NH encountered Confederate soldiers entrenched upon the ridge surrounding a church, intense fighting broke out. A minie-ball struck my great-great grandfather in the chest, one and one-fourth inches below the right nipple. The ball traveled through his body, ranging downward and lodged against the skin about a half inch right of his backbone, where it was taken out by an Army Surgeon the day after he was shot.

Transferred to Carver Hospital in Washington DC my grandfather recuperated there for two months. He was honorably discharged with a Surgeon's Certificate of Disability June 5, 1865, and went home to his wife and children back in Franklin County, PA."

Near Farmville, VA   *Photo provided by author*

This narrative is a shorter version of the facts, events and experiences, I've compiled about my great-great grandfather's Civil War service. Yours can be as long or as short as you like. Use descriptive words that get to the essence of his experience. Fill in around the facts with some of the background information you've gathered from your reading. Remember this is your ancestor's story. You want to honor him so don't get bogged down worrying about writing perfection. The idea is to shake the dust off your Civil War ancestor, use the important dates and places in his life, and put them in sequence adding up to the real, living, breathing person he was. Make this a tribute to your family member who experienced some of the most turbulent times this nation has ever seen, who had an impact on his country and on the lives of his descendants. Make this memorial something you'll read again and again and share with your family.

Good luck and enjoy the benefits of your research!

Appendix A

Glossary

amnesty - Pardon granted to a large group of people.

artillery - A branch of the army that used large caliber guns, cannons and mortars.

brigade - Consisted of three to six regiments and led by a brigadier general.

cavalry - a branch of an army who rode on horseback. They were used for scouting and gaining info regarding their enemy, many times the first to participate in battle.

commissions – A group given the authority to perform certain functions.
Confederate - Those loyal to the Confederate States of America, rebel, southerner.

company – A military unit made up of approximately 100 men and led by a captain. Ten companies made a regiment.

corps – Comprised of two or more divisions led by a lieutenant general in the Confederate army or a major general in the Union army.

cutter Guard – the predecessor of today's Coast Guard, cutter is a type of boat.

division – Made up of three or four brigades in the Union army and commanded by a major general. A division in the Confederacy had four to six brigades.

infantry - a branch of an army, soldiers that travel and fight on foot.

muster – To officially enter the military, or roll call.

pension – A fixed sum of money paid regularly to a person following retirement from military service or to their surviving dependents. Union Civil War pensions were paid by the federal government. Confederate Civil War pensions were paid by the individual southern states.

regiment – A military unit made up of ten companies (about 1,000 men) and led by a colonel.

secession – the official act of withdrawing, as when the southern states separated from the United States in 1861.

union – Those loyal to the United States government, northerner.

State Archives for Further Research

Alabama Department of Archives and History
624 Washington Avenue, Montgomery, AL 36130
P.O. Box 300100, Montgomery, AL 36130
Phone: (334) 242-4435
Website: http://www.archives.alabama.gov/

Arkansas History Commission
One Capitol Mall, Little Rock, AR 77201
Phone: (501) 682-6900
Website: http://www.ark-ives.com/

Kentucky Department for Library and Archives
P.O. Box 537, Frankfort, KY 40601
Phone: (502) 564-8300
Website: http://kdla.ky.gov/Pages/default.aspx

State Archives of Florida
R.A. Gray Building, 500 South Bronough Street, Tallahassee, FL 32399-0250
Phone: (850) 245-6700
Website: http://dlis.dos.state.fl.us/index_researchers.cfm

Georgia Archives
5800 Jonesboro Road, Morrow, GA 30260
Phone: (678) 364-3700
Website: http://www.georgiaarchives.org

Louisiana State Archives
3851 Essen Lane, Baton Rouge, LA 70809
Phone: (225) 922-1000
Website: http://www.sos.la.gov/HistoricalResources/LearnAboutTheArchives/Pages/default.aspx

Mississippi Department of Archives and History
P.O. Box 571, Jackson, MS 39205-0571
Phone: (601) 576-6876
Website: http://mdah.state.ms.us/

Missouri State Archives
600 W. Main, P.O. Box 1747, Jefferson City, MO 65102
Phone: (573) 751-3280
Website: http://www.sos.mo.gov/archives/

North Carolina State Archives
4614 Mail Service Center, Raleigh, NC 27699-4614
Phone: (919) 807-7310
Website: http://www.archives.ncdcr.gov

South Carolina Department of Archives and History
8301 Parklane Road, Columbia, SC 29223
Phone: (803) 896-6104
Website: http://scdah.sc.gov/

Tennessee State Library and Archives
403 7th Avenue North, Nashville, TN 37243
Phone: (615) 741-2764
Website: http://www.tennessee.gov/tsla/

Texas State Library and Archives Commission
P.O. Box 12927, Austin, TX 78711-2927
Phone: (512) 463-5455
Website: http://www.tsl.state.tx.us/

Library of Virginia
800 East Broad Street, Richmond, VA 23219
Phone: (804) 692-3500
Website: http://www.lva.virginia.gov/

West Virginia State Archives
Archives and History Library
The Cultural Center, 1900 Kanawha Boulevard East, Charleston, WV 25305-0300
Phone: (304) 558-0230
Website: http://www.wvculture.org/history/wvsamenu.html

A complete list of all State Archives and contact information may be found on NARA (http://www.archives.gov/research/alic/reference/state-archives.html and the Council of State Archivists at http://www.statearchivists.org/states.htm.

Regimental "Cheat Sheet"

_____   _____

Corps   Commanding Officer

_____   _____

Division   Commanding Officer

_____   _____

Brigade   Commanding Officer

_____   _____

Regiment   Commanding Officer

_____   _____

Other regiments in brigade   Commanding Officer

_____

Other regiments in brigade

_____

Commanding Officer

_____

Other regiments in brigade

_____

Commanding Officer

_____

Other regiments in brigade

_____

Commanding Officer

_____

Other regiments in brigade

_____

Commanding Officer

Appendix D

Resources for Civil War Research

Extended Civil War Research

This list is in addition to those publications referenced within the book.

Crute, Joseph H., *Units of the Confederate States Army.* Midlothian VA: Derwent Books, 1987.

Dyer, Frederick H. A, *Compendium of the War of the Rebellion.* 3 vols. New York: Thomas Yoseloff, 1959. Reprint. Dayton: Press of Morningside, 1994.

Hewitt, Janet B., *Supplement to the Official Records of the Union and Confederate Armies.* 95 vols, Wilmington, NC: Broadfoot Publishing Company, 1994 – 1998.

Sigakis, Stewart. *Compendium of the Confederate Armies.* 11 vols. New York: Facts on File, 1992-97.

The Union Army. 8 vols. Madison, WI: Federal Publishing Company, 1908. Reprinted in 9 vols. Wilmington, NC: Broadfoot Publishing Company, 1998.

United Confederate Veterans. *List of Organized Camps of the United Confederate Veterans.* New Orleans: Rogers' Printing Co., 1921.

U.S. Naval War Records Office. *Register of Officers of the Confederate States Navy 1861 – 1865.* Washington D.C. Government Printing Office, 1931.

U.S. Naval War Records Office. *War of the Rebellion: A Compilation of the Official Records of the Union and Confederate Navies.* 30 volumes. Washington D.C. Government Printing

Office, 1874 – 1922.

U.S. War Department. *Atlas to Accompany the Official Records of the War of the Rebellion.* Washington D.C. Government Printing Office, 1891 – 1895.

Wright, John. *Compendium of the Confederacy.* 2 vols. Wilmington, NC: Broadfoot Publishing Company, 1998.

Yoseloff, Thomas, *The Photographic History of the Civil War.* 10 vols. New York: Review of Reviews Company, 1911. Reprint. 5 vols. New York: Blue and Grey Press, William H. Taft, 1997.

Books For Your Nightstand

Battle Cry of Freedom by James McPherson

Black Southerners in Confederate Armies: A Collection of Historical Accounts by J. H. Segars and Charles Kelly Barrow

A Blaze of Glory: A Novel of the Battle of Shiloh by Jeff Shaara

The Civil War in Color: A Photographic Reenactment of the War Between the States by John C. Guntzelman

The Civil War Research Guide by Stephen McManus

Co. Aytch: A Confederate Memoir of the Civil War by Samuel R. Watkins

Hard Tack and Coffee: Soldiers Life in the Civil War by John D. Billings

In Search of Your Confederate Ancestors by J. H. Segars

Landscape Turned Red: The Battle of Antietam by Stephen W. Sears

The Sable Arm: Black Troops in the Union Army, 1861-1865 by Dudley Taylor Cornish

A Stillness at Appomattox by Bruce Catton

Tracing Your Civil War Ancestor by Bertram Hawthorne Groene

Additional Websites for Civil War Research

African American Civil War Memorial and Museum - http://www.afroamcivilwar.org/

African American Gateway - http://www.genealogycenter.info/africanamerican/results_afram.php?subject=Military

African American Soldiers during the Civil War - http://www.loc.gov/teachers/classroommaterials/presentationsandactivities/presentations/timeline/civilwar/aasoldrs/

Civil War - http://www.civilwar.com/

The Civil War Archive http://www.civilwararchive.com/

The Civil War Center at Louisiana State University - http://www.lib.lsu.edu/cwc/

The Civil War Home Page - http://www.civil-war.net/

Civil War Soldier Search http://www.civilwarsoldiersearch.com/

Civil War Trust - http://www.civilwar.org/

Confederate Research Sources - http://search.ancestry.com/search/db.aspx?dbid=3207

Confederate States Navy - http://csnavy.org/

Cyndi's List - http://www.cyndislist.com/

Military History Online http://www.militaryhistoryonline.com/civilwar/

The National Civil War Museum - http://www.nationalcivilwarmuseum.org/

National Civil War Naval Museum - http://portcolumbus.org/

National Park Systems Historical and Genealogical Research http://www.nps.gov/frsp/archive.htm

Official Records of the Union and Confederate Navies - http://wtj.com/archives/acwnavies/

Shotgun's Home of the American Civil War - http://www.civilwarhome.com/

Sons of the Confederacy - http://www.scv.org/

Sons of Union Veterans - http://www.suvcw.org/

Thomas Legion: The 69th North Carolina Regiment - http://thomaslegion.net/index.html

Index

The In-Depth Genealogist is a digital community that contributes to the advancement of all genealogists.

As a free genealogy community, The In-Depth Genealogist provides a variety of services. A monthly digital magazine, a monthly email newsletter, and hosts #IDGchat on Twitter. It has an active blog which provides articles and columns for the advancement of all genealogists, professional or non-professional. We pride ourselves on sharing our knowledge and experience in a friendly, approachable, and entertaining way. Go in-depth with us! Please make sure to find us on you social media of choice, **Facebook**, **Twitter**, **Google** + and **YouTube**.

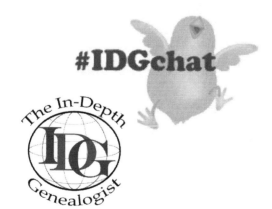

You asked, we answered with #IDGchat on the first and third Friday of the month at 8 pm EST/ 7 CST. Check out our schedule with topics at http://theindepthgenealogist.com/idgchat/

Our IDG Publications

Going In-Depth is a free monthly magazine released

on the 15th of each month.

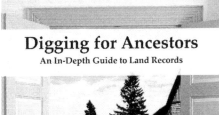

"Digging for Ancestors" is available

for download in PDF, Kindle, and

Nook formats.

Or get the 8.5" x 11" Full

Color Paperback